A WORDSWORTH HANDBOOK

MILITARY INSIGNIA

Wordsworth Editions

First published in England 1995 by
Wordsworth Editions Ltd
Cumberland House
Crib Street
Ware
Hertfordshire SG12 9ET

ISBN 1–85326–820–8

Previous page: **the United Nations flag flies in the background above a
parade of peacekeeping force personnel from Sweden, the UK, Canada,
Denmark, Finland and Ireland**

Designed and produced by Superlaunch Ltd
P O Box 207, Abingdon, Oxfordshire OX13 6TA, England
Text conversion and pagination by
August Filmsetting, St Helens, England
Colour separation, printing and binding
in the Czech Republic by Svoboda

NOTE

Bosnia, Croatia, Macedonia and Slovenia are entered under 'former Yugoslavia'. The Commonwealth of Independent States (CIS) comprises Armenia, Azerbaijan, Belarus, Kazakhstan, Kirghizia, Moldova, Russia, Tadjikistan, Turkmenistan, Ukraine, Uzbekistan. Georgia is not joining the CIS but is included there for convenience; the Independent Baltic States are Latvia, Estonia and Lithuania. For Zaïre, see Congo-Kinshasa; and for Burma, see Myanmar.

Full details of the entire organisation of each of the forces described cannot be included owing to restrictions on the space available, but some indications of size are provided within the various organisations

Below: *Long Beach Naval Shipyard, California; a crewman sews a battleship* USS New Jersey *patch to his jacket, upon completion of the ship's recommissioning ceremony, December 1982*

AFGHANISTAN

Army
Personnel: 50,000+
Organisation: 13 infantry divisions, 3 armoured divisions, 1 mountain infantry division, 1 artillery brigade, 3 artillery regiments, 4 commando regiments and 1 parachute battalion
Equipment: 660 MBTs and 600 AIFVs and APCs

Air Force
Personnel: 7,500+
Organisation: 3 fighter, 10 fighter bomber and 5 helicopter squadrons, plus transport, liaison and trainer aircraft

ALBANIA

Navy
Personnel: 3,300 including 1,000 conscripts serving for 36 months
Fleet: 2 submarines plus patrol and light forces

Army
Personnel: 31,500 including 20,000 conscripts serving for 24 months
Organisation: 1 tank and 4 infantry brigades
Equipment: 100 tanks, 80 APCs

Air Force
Personnel: 7,200 including 1,400 conscripts serving for 36 months
Organisation: combat command with 7 fighter ground attack squadrons, transport command and helicopter command with 1 squadron and trainer command

ALGERIA

Navy
Personnel: 6,400
Fleet: 3 frigates, 6 corvettes, 2 submarines, 25 fast attack craft, 6 patrol boats, 4 training craft, 1 mine warfare vessel and other amphibious forces and miscellaneous craft

Army
Personnel: 125,000 including 85,000 conscripts serving for 24 months
Organisation: 2 armoured divisions, 2 mechanised divisions, 9 motorised infantry brigades, 1 airborne brigade, 30 independent infantry battalions and independent artillery battalions, 4 engineer battalions and 2 ranger battalions
Equipment: 745 MBTs, 169 armoured cars and 1,500 AIFVs and APCs

Air Force
Personnel: 12,000

4

Organisation: combat command with 8 fighter, 5 fighter ground attack and 1 recce squadron; other commands are transport, helicopters, liaison and training and maritime patrol

ANGOLA

Navy
Personnel: 1,500
Fleet: 6 FACs, 2 mine sweepers, 4 torpedo boats and 7 patrol craft

Army
Personnel: 53,500
Organisation: 10 military regions each with 6 infantry brigades of battalion strength
Equipment: 187 MBTs and 272 APCs

Air Force
Personnel: 5,000
Fleet: 91 fighter aircraft, 63 transports, 3 maritime patrol aircraft, 25 trainers and 90 helicopters

ARGENTINA

Navy
Personnel: 25,000 including 6,000 conscripts serving for 14 months
Fleet: 1 aircraft carrier, 6 destroyers, 7 frigates, 2 submarines, 6 patrol craft,

light forces and landing forces. There are 6 non-operational mine sweepers

Naval Aviation
Personnel: 2,000
Organisation: 6 wings; 1 attack, 1 ASW and 4 marine recce squadrons

Marines
Personnel: 5,000
Organisation: 1 marine brigade with 2 infantry battalions, 1 amphibious support force and 1 marine force

Army
Personnel: 41,000 including 13,000 conscripts serving for 12 months
Organisation: 4 army corps, each covering its own area, with a total of 10 brigades
Equipment: 306 MBTs, 106 tank destroyers, 728 APCs and other AFVs including 3 M.577 command post vehicles

Army Aviation
Fleet: 85 fixed and rotary wing aircraft

Air Force
Personnel: 13,000 including 1,500 conscripts serving for 12 months
Organisation: Air Operations Command with 9 air brigades and 1 anti-aircraft group

Argentine paratroop wings

comprising 6 transport, 9 fighter bomber, 3 COIN, 3 helicopter, 1 photo recce and 1 bomber squadron

AUSTRALIA

An airman wears a patch commemorating the joint Australian, New Zealand and US Triad '84 exercise

Navy
Personnel: 14,720
Fleet: 3 destroyers, 8 frigates, 5 submarines, 2 mine hunters, 1 mine sweeper and 17 patrol craft, together with survey ships, miscellaneous craft and other amphibious vessels

Naval Aviation
Personnel: 950
Organisation: 3 units with 32 helicopters

Army
Personnel: 31,252
Organisation: land force command, logistic command and training command; the land force command comprises in the main 3 divisional HQs and 10 brigade HQs. There is 1 ground liaison group and 34 regiments, 22 battalions and 52 squadrons
Equipment: 103 MBTs and 700 APCs

Air Force
Personnel: 18,427
Organisation: air command, logistics command and training command are the 3

Below: *the insignia of the Australian Special Air Service Regiment*

major commands in line with Army thinking. There are 2 strike recce, 4 tactical fighter, 2 maritime recce and 4 transport squadrons

Above: *the aircraft insignia of the Royal Australian Air Force*

AUSTRIA

Army
Personnel: 46,000
Organisation: in field units including artillery, guard, special forces and anti-tank battalions
Equipment: 169 MBTs, 234 tank destroyers and 460 APCs

Air Force
Personnel: 6,000 including 2,400 conscripts
Organisation: 3 air regiments and 3 air defence battalions

Right: *an Austrian representative of UN Command*

BAHAMAS, THE

Navy
Personnel: 870
Fleet: 15 patrol craft and 2 supply support vessels

Naval Aviation
Fleet: 5 aircraft

BAHRAIN

Navy
Personnel: 650 plus 250 coast guard
Fleet: 2 corvettes, 8 fast attack craft, 30 coastal patrol craft of the coast guard, 1 landing

craft, 1 hovercraft and 5 armed launches

Army

Personnel: 5,000
Organisation: 1 infantry brigade, 1 armoured battalion, 1 artillery battalion and 1 special forces battalion
Equipment: 54 MBTs, 149 APCs and 40 armoured cars

Air Force

Personnel: 460
Organisation: 2 fighter and 1 helicopter squadron

BANGLADESH

Navy

Personnel: 8,000
Fleet: 4 frigates, 8 FACs, 31 patrol boats and 4 torpedo boats

Army

Personnel: 90,000
Organisation: 6 infantry division HQs, 14 infantry brigades, 2 armoured regiments, 6 artillery regiments and 7 engineer battalions
Equipment: 87 MBTs

Air Force

Personnel: 6,000
Organisation: 2 fighter, 2 fighter ground attack, 1 transport and 2 helicopter squadrons

BELGIUM

Navy

Personnel: 4,250 including 1,160 conscripts
Fleet: 4 frigates, 16 mine warfare craft and 3 helicopters of Naval Aviation

Army

Personnel: 53,530 including 23,000 conscripts, but to be reduced by 1995
Organisation: 6 brigades including 1 para commando brigade, 12 battalions including 4 engineer battalions, and 3 light aviation squadrons
Equipment: 334 MBTs, 236 AIFVs, 889 APCs and 286 other AFVs; Army Aviation has 10 fixed and 92 rotary wing aircraft

Air Force

Personnel: 17,631 including 4,500 conscripts

Top right: *a commando regiment cap badge of the Belgian paratroops*

Centre right: *the current insignia of the 3rd Paratroop, Belgium*

Bottom right: *current Belgian Air Defence highly élite cross trained unit insignia*

Organisation: 4 fighter ground attack, 2 air defence, 1 recce and 2 transport squadrons; this is to be reduced to 5-6 squadrons by 1995, deployed in 3 wings

BELIZE

Navy
Personnel: 50
Fleet: 10 patrol craft

Army
Personnel: 600
Organisation: 1 infantry battalion

Air Force
Personnel: 50
Fleet: 3 aircraft

BENIN

Navy
Personnel: 150
Fleet: 2 craft

Army
Personnel: 3,650
Organisation: 5 battalions with 1 commando company, 1 artillery battery and 1 armoured squadron
Equipment: 20 light tanks and 27 armoured cars

Air Force
Personnel: 200
Organisation: 1 transport unit

BOLIVIA

Navy
Personnel: 4,000 including 550 marines
Fleet: 20 lake patrol craft and 1 transport vessel

Naval Aviation
Fleet: 4 aircraft

Army
Personnel: 23,000 including 19,000 conscripts
Organisation: 6 military regions; 10 divisions, comprised mostly of 22 infantry battalions
Equipment: 36 tank destroyers, 24 armoured cars and 98 APCs

Army Aviation
Fleet: 8 aircraft

A Bolivian pilot's uniform patch, Santa Cruz de la Sierra, Bolivia, May 1986

Air Force
Personnel: 4,000
Organisation: 4 air brigades comprised mostly of 4 fighter air groups, 5 tactical air groups and 2 transport groups

The Bolivian Air Transport insignia

The Bolivian Special Forces badge

BOTSWANA

Defence Force
Personnel: 5,800
Organisation: 2 infantry brigades with 1 armoured car battalion
Equipment: 12 armoured cars and 38 APCs; the Air Wing has 1 attack unit and 1 transport liaison unit

BRAZIL

Navy
Personnel: 50,000 including 15,000 marines
Fleet: 1 aircraft carrier, 6 destroyers, 14 frigates, 6 submarines and 7 patrol craft; plus light forces, amphibious forces and 6 mine sweepers

Naval Aviation
Organisation: 5 helicopter squadrons with a fleet of 65 helicopters

Marines
Organisation: 1 amphibious division, 1 reinforcement command, and 1 independent special operations group

Army
Personnel: 196,000 including 145,000 conscripts serving for 12 months
Organisation: 7 military commands are responsible for 12 military regions with operational units at brigade level including 28 artillery groups and 12 motorised infantry brigades
Equipment: 520 light tanks and 797 APCs

Army Aviation
Fleet: 52 helicopters

Air Force
Personnel: 50,700
Organisation: Air Defence Command, Tactical Command, Coastal Command, Transport Command and Training Command

BRUNEI

Navy
Personnel: 680
Fleet: 3 FACs, 9 patrol craft and 20 other small launches and river craft; the naval air arm has a fleet of 3 maritime patrol aircraft

Army
Personnel: 3,600
Organisation: 3 infantry battalions, 1 support battalion, 1 special forces and 1 armoured recce squadron, 1 air defence battery and 1 engineer group
Equipment: 16 MBTs and 26 APCs

Air Force
Personnel: 300
Organisation: 1 COIN and 3 helicopter transport liaison squadrons

BULGARIA

Navy
Personnel: 9,000 including 4,500 conscripts
Fleet: 2 frigates, 3 submarines, 9 patrol craft, 12 mine sweepers, plus light forces and landing craft

Army
Personnel: 75,000 including 50,000 conscripts
Organisation: 12 regiments, 4 tank brigades and 4 motorised rifle divisions
Equipment: about 1,500 tanks and 2,000 AIFVs and APCs

Air Force
Personnel: 22,000 including 15,000 conscripts serving for 18 months
Organisation: combat command includes 4 interceptor regiments, transport command, helicopter command and training

BURKINA FASO

Defence Force
Personnel: 8,000
Organisation: 5 infantry and 1 paratroop regiment with 3 battalions, all at very low strength
Equipment: 71 armoured cars

Air Wing
Personnel: 500
Organisation: 1 fighter ground attack unit and 1 transport unit

BURUNDI

Defence Force
Personnel: 6,800
Organisation: 4 battalions
Equipment: 16 armoured cars and 16 APCs

Air Wing
Personnel: 150
Fleet: 4 fixed and 13 rotary wing aircraft

CAMBODIA

Navy
Personnel: 900
Fleet: 2 patrol hydrofoils and 10 patrol craft

Army
Personnel: 40,000
Organisation: 6 infantry divisions, 3 independent infantry regiments, 1 cavalry regiment and 4 tank battalions
Equipment: 91 MBTs and 130 APCs

Air Force

Organisation: 2 fighter squadrons plus fixed wing transports and 12 helicopters

CAMEROUN

Navy

Personnel: 1,400
Fleet: 2 FACs, 4 patrol boats, 30 river boats and 8 landing craft

Army

Personnel: 6,000
Organisation: 9 battalions with engineer and support units
Equipment: 21 armoured cars and 42 APCs

Air Force

Personnel: 300
Organisation: 1 fighter ground attack squadron, together with transport, liaison aircraft and helicopters

CANADA

In order to make reference and comparison easy within this book, the Canadian forces have been defined in the traditional manner; however, in reality they have a unified structure which does not distinguish between the services. Organisation is into five functional commands: mobile, maritime, communications, air, and training.

Navy

Personnel: being reorganised as 10,000 regulars plus reserves
Organisation: task groups based on the Atlantic and Pacific coasts
Fleet: 6 destroyers, 11 frigates and 3 submarines, together with miscellaneous auxiliaries; the coast guard operates 110 unarmed vessels

Army

Personnel: 20,500 regulars
Organisation: 3 brigade groups, each with its own HQ, 3 infantry battalions, 1 armoured regiment, 1 artillery regiment, 1 engineer regiment, 1 service battalion, 1 field ambulance, 1 signal squadron, 1 military police platoon and 1 intelligence platoon
Equipment: 114 MBTs, 174 armoured cars, 1,149 AIFVs and APCs

A soldier of the Royal Canadian Dragoons on UN duty

The cap badge of the Royal Canadian 22e Regiment

A 435th (T) Transportation Squadron patch on the shoulder of a member of the Canadian armed forces. The squadron flies resupply missions to 30 radar stations on the Distant Early Warning Line, which runs from Alaska across northern Canada to Greenland

Air Force

Personnel: 18,500

Organisation: the Air Force (Air Command) is organised into 6 groups, fighter, maritime, tactical, transport, training and air reserve, with 4 air defence, 2 ground attack and 2 composite squadrons to cover combat support, electronic warfare training, coastal patrol and arms control verification; 3 maritime patrol and 2 maritime helicopter squadrons and training units, 1 helicopter squadron for emergency response teams (SERT), 1 strategic transport, VIP and refuelling, 1 transport and 4 SAR squadrons and a rescue unit

CAPE VERDE

Navy

Personnel: 90

Fleet: 6 vessels

Army

Personnel: 1,000
Organisation: 1 infantry battalion and 1 ranger company

Air Force

Personnel: 65
Fleet: 3 aircraft

CENTRAL AFRICAN REPUBLIC

Army

Personnel: 3,500
Organisation: 1 infantry regiment, 1 republican guard regiment and 2 battalions and 1 engineer company
Equipment: 4 MBTs, 48 armoured cars and 4 APCs; the river patrol force has a strength of 100 men and 9 patrol craft

Air Force

Personnel: 300
Fleet: 17 transport liaison aircraft and 2 helicopters

CHAD

Army

Personnel: 25,500
Equipment: 57 armoured cars

Air Force

Personnel: 240
Fleet: 4 combat aircraft, 10 transports, 4 helicopters and 7 liaison aircraft

CHILE

Navy

Personnel: 26,000 including 2,000 conscripts serving for 24 months
Organisation: four naval zones
Fleet: 6 destroyers, 8 frigates and 4 submarines, plus light forces

Naval Aviation

Personnel: 600
Organisation: 4 squadrons

Marines

Personnel: 4,200
Organisation: 4 detachments each with 1 reinforced infantry battalion, 1 command company, 1 combat diver company, 1 field artillery battery and 1 anti-aircraft artillery battery

Army

Personnel: 55,000 including 30,000 conscripts serving for 12 months
Organisation: 6 divisions and 1 independent brigade
Equipment: 221 MBTs, 107 light tanks, 230 armoured cars and nearly 200 APCs

Army Aviation

Organisation: 1 regiment under

Army Command plus independent aviation sections attached to divisions
Fleet: 94 fixed and rotary wing aircraft

Air Force
Personnel: 14,000
Organisation: four air brigades; squadrons include 1 interceptor, 1 ground attack, 1 fighter ground attack and 1 ground attack close support

CHINA (PRC)

Strategic Forces (Rocket Units)
Personnel: 90,000
Organisation: 7 divisions, organised into brigades, regiments and battalions of varying sizes
Equipment: apart from missiles, Strategic Forces has a fleet of 4 SSBN submarines

Navy
Personnel: 185,000
Organisation: Naval High Command directs the three fleets (North Sea, East Sea and South Sea), plus Naval Aviation and coastal defence forces
Fleet: 20 destroyers, 14 frigates, 115 submarines, 500 FACs of which 180 carry missiles, 68 patrol craft, 110 patrol hydrofoils, 80 torpedo boats, 300+ small patrol boats, 23

A Chinese People's Navy patch

mine sweepers and other amphibious forces and supply ships

Naval Aviation
Personnel: 38,000
Organisation: 3 bomber anti-ship strike air divisions, 6 fighter ground attack air divisions and transports and helicopters, including maritime patrol and ASW

Marines
Personnel: 38,000
Organisation: 5 marine infantry regiments, and special forces

Army
Personnel: 2,300,000
Organisation: 29 military districts make up 7 military regions, with 24 combined

A Chinese People's Liberation Army patch

forces army groups (corps), which include 5 rapid deployment groups totalling 85 infantry divisions, 10 armoured mechanised divisions, 3 airborne divisions, 10 artillery divisions, 1 mountain division, 50 independent engineer regiments, 19 signal regiments plus special forces
Equipment: 10,000 MBTs and 5,000 APCs

Air Force
Personnel: 470,000 including 220,000 air defence
Organisation: 7 air districts, each with a defence force, which operate independently; each aircraft division has 2-5 regiments. In total there are 200 fighter and fighter ground

attack, 120 strike fighter, 42 bomber and 50 transport squadrons, plus 260+ recce aircraft, 1,000+ trainers and 400+ helicopters

COLOMBIA

Navy
Personnel: 13,000
Organisation: in four commands
Fleet: 4 frigates and 4 submarines, plus light forces of river gunboats and patrol craft; Naval Aviation has 3 squadrons with fixed and rotary wing aircraft

A patch worn by the Colombian Air Force personnel participating in an international disaster relief effort, following a volcanic eruption; Palanquero Air Force Base, Colombia, November 1985

Marines
Personnel: 6,000

Army
Personnel: 115,000 including 35,000 conscripts serving for 24 months
Organisation: 4 divisions (13 brigades) covering 10 military regions
Equipment: 45 tanks and 370 + AFVs

Air Force
Personnel: 7,000 including 2,000 conscripts serving for 12 months
Organisation: 4 commands; combat (includes 2 fighter ground attack squadrons), tactical support, transport and training

COMMONWEALTH OF INDEPENDENT STATES (CIS)
(Armenia, Azerbaijan, Belarus, Kazakhstan, Kirghizia, Moldova, Russia, Tadjikistan, Turkmenistan, Ukraine, Uzbekistan; Georgia is not joining the CIS but is included here for convenience; the Independent Baltic States are Latvia, Estonia and Lithuania)

Navy
Personnel: 333,000
Organisation: four main fleets; Black Sea, Baltic, Pacific and

A United Nations Iraq-Kuwait Observation Unit (UNIKOM) soldier from the USSR greeting a young shepherd at the southern Iraq-Kuwaiti border, May 1991

A Soviet Naval Infantry patch

Northern, of which both the Pacific and the Northern are completely under CIS (Russian) control, and have recently been strengthened. The Black Sea Fleet is currently under joint Russian Ukrainian control, but this is expected to end soon with a split between Russia and the Ukraine, which will result in the formation of two new navies
Fleet: 1 non-operational aircraft carrier, 2 V/STOL aircraft carriers, 1 non-operational helicopter cruiser, 55 SSBN submarines of which 42 are being scrapped, 35 SSN submarines of which 10 are being withdrawn, 83 SSN torpedo submarines of which 8 are being withdrawn, 90 patrol submarines some of which are being withdrawn, 25 cruisers, 38 destroyers, 35 frigates, 220 corvettes, 74 light forces including patrol hydrofoils, fast attack craft hydrofoils, 383 mine warfare forces and amphibious forces, air cushion vehicles and major auxiliaries and support ships

Naval Air Arm
Personnel: 65,000
Organisation: four fleet air forces correspond to the four naval fleets, and are responsible for shipborne rotary and V/STOL fixed wing aircraft deployed as bombers naval strike, ASW, fighters, transports, recce EW targetting and helicopters

Naval Aviation
Organisation: separate to the Naval Air Arm and responsible for shore based aircraft only
Fleet: 900 fixed and 200 rotary wing aircraft

Naval Infantry
Personnel: 15,000 plus 7,000 coastal artillery and rocket troops

Army
Equipment: (totals as held in the former Soviet Union) 37,000 MBTs, 2,400 armoured cars, 76,700 AIVFs and APCs, plus the Army Aviation fleet of 4,300 helicopters

A Soviet Motor Rifle Regiment patch

The Soviet Airborne Regiment

Air Force

Fleet: (totals as held in the former Soviet Union) 2,000 fighters, 2,500 tactical combat aircraft, 1,000 bombers, 600 recce aircraft, 500 electronic warfare ELINT aircraft, 3,500 transport aircraft, 100 aerial tankers, 7,000 trainers and 1,500 armed helicopters

Agreements regarding arms distribution to individual States were made in 1992, as follows:

Armenia
Personnel: no set ceiling
Organisation: 220 MBTs, 220 AFVs, 100 combat aircraft and 50 armed helicopters

Azerbaijan
Personnel: no set ceiling
Organisation: 220 MBTs, 220 AFVs, 100 combat aircraft and 50 armed helicopters

Belarus
Personnel: 100,000 army and air force
Equipment: 1,800 MBTs, 2,600 AFVs, 260 combat aircraft and 80 armed helicopters

Georgia
Personnel: 40,000 army and air force
Equipment: 220 MBTs, 220 AFVs, 100 combat aircraft and 50 armed helicopters

Moldova
Personnel: no set ceiling
Equipment: 210 MBTs, 210 AFVs, 50 combat aircraft and

A current CIS MVD Ministry of the Interior patch

50 armed helicopters
Russia (European part only)
Personnel: 1,450,000 army and air force
Equipment: 6,400 MBTs, 11,480 AFVs, 3,450 combat aircraft and 890 armed helicopters
Ukraine
Personnel: 450,000 army and air force
Equipment: 4,080 MBTs, 5,050 AFVs, 1,090 combat aircraft and 330 armed helicopters

Air Force Organisation

Note: this applied to the former Soviet Air Force and is the model on which the new Russian Air Force is based
Military transport aviation
Long range aviation: bombers, fighters and strike aircraft
Frontal aviation: fighter, strike and ground attack
Aviation of the Air Defence Force (a separate service): fighters and interceptors
Naval Aviation (parts only): *see above*

Air Defence Force

Organisation: space surveillance force (PKO); rocket defence troops (PRO); air defence rocket zenith rocket troops (ZRV); fighter force (APVO) and radar technical troops (RV-PRO)
Fleet: 2,435 interceptors, 20 AWACS and 350 trainers

CONGO

Navy
Personnel: 200
Fleet: 10 patrol craft

Army
Personnel: 10,000
Organisation: 7 battalions and 1 artillery group
Equipment: 51 MBTs, 24 armoured cars and 79 APCs

Air Force
Personnel: 500
Fleet: 31 combat aircraft, 10 transports and 5 helicopters

CONGO-KINSHASA

Navy
(responsible for coast, rivers and lakes)
Personnel: 2,300 including 600 marines
Fleet: 14 patrol craft

Army
Personnel: 28,000
Organisation: 3 regional HQs, 1 infantry division, 2 para commando brigades, 1 armoured brigade, 1 presidential guard division, 1 special forces group
Equipment: 64 MTBs, 115 armoured cars and 96 APCs

Air Force
Personnel: 2,500

Organisation: 1 fighter, 2 COIN and 1 helicopter squadron and 15 transports and 36 trainers

CÔTE D'IVOIRE

Navy
Personnel: 800
Fleet: 2 fast attack craft, 2 patrol craft and 1 landing ship

Army
Personnel: 6,300
Organisation: 4 battalions
Equipment: 5 light tanks and 47 armoured cars

Air Force
Personnel: 800
Organisation: 1 fighter ground attack squadron, plus transport and liaison aircraft and helicopters

A Cuban tank specialist badge

CUBA

Navy
Personnel: 13,000 including 8,500 conscripts
Fleet: 3 frigates, 1 corvette, 3 submarines, 34 patrol craft and 11 mine sweepers

Army
Personnel: 145,000 including 60,000 conscripts
Organisation: 4 regional commands which include 13 infantry divisions and 3 armoured divisions
Equipment: over 1,500 tanks and 1,150 AIFVs and APCs

Air Force
Personnel: 20,000 including 11,000 conscripts
Organisation: 5 commands; combat (includes 5 fighter and 2 fighter bomber squadrons), transport, training, helicopter and air defence

CYPRUS

National Guard of the Republic of Cyprus
Personnel: 10,000; conscription is for 24 months
Organisation: 1 armoured brigade, 13 infantry battalions and 7 artillery battalions
Equipment: 54 MBTs, 186 APCs and 160 armoured cars; there is also a naval service with 1 coastal patrol craft

Turkish Cypriot Security Police
Personnel: 4,500; conscription is for 24 months
Organisation: 7 infantry battalions

CZECH AND SLOVAKIAN REPUBLICS

Army
Personnel: 65,500
Organisation: the 3 military commands established in 1992 have now been disbanded
Equipment: 1,440 MBTs and 2,050 AIFVs and APCs

Air Force
Personnel: 46,200 including 17,000 air defence troops
Organisation: 1 combined air corps, 3 air defence divisions, 3 air school regiments and 1 air transport regiment

DENMARK

Navy
Personnel: 5,000 including 900 conscripts
Fleet: 3 frigates, 5 submarines, 6 mine layers and 3 mine sweepers, patrol craft and light forces; Naval Aviation has 8 helicopters

Army
Personnel: 17,400 including 8,500 conscripts
Organisation: 1 geographical command, 2 divisional HQs, 5 mechanised infantry brigades; each brigade has 1 tank, 2

Left: *an arm badge of the Czech Republic Airborne Regiment*

mechanised, and 1 artillery battalion
Equipment: 380 MBTs, 384 APCs and Army Aviation has 28 helicopters

Air Force
Personnel: 6,600 including 800 conscripts
Organisation: tactical air

Above: *the current Army badge of the Czech Republic*

command in 4 major air bases, each with a fighter ground attack squadron, plus air matériel command

Overleaf: *a 1982 arm patch of the Danish Army*

25

DJIBOUTI

Navy
Personnel: 100
Fleet: 6 patrol craft

Army
Personnel: 2,600
Organisation: 2 regional commands with 1 infantry regiment, 1 armoured squadron, 1 support battalion, 1 border commando battalion and 1 parachute company
Equipment: 52 armoured cars and 12 APCs

Air Force
Personnel: 80
Organisation: 1 transport and 1 helicopter squadron

DOMINICAN REPUBLIC, THE

Navy
Personnel: 4,600

Fleet: 1 frigate and 5 corvettes, plus light forces and 1 landing craft

Naval Air Arm
Fleet: 9 aircraft

Army
Personnel: 13,900
Organisation: 5 defence zones, including 4 infantry brigades (17 battalions)
Equipment: 14 light tanks, 63 armoured cars and 20 APCs

Army Aviation
Fleet: 173 aircraft

Air Force
Personnel: 3,800
Organisation: 3 commands, combat, training and helicopters

ECUADOR

Navy
Personnel: 5,000
Fleet: 2 frigates, 6 corvettes and 2 submarines, plus light forces including 4 landing craft

Naval Aviation
Personnel: 200
Organisation: 15 aircraft

Marines
Personnel: 1,900
Organisation: 3 battalions

Army

Personnel: 48,500
Organisation: 4 military zones are covered by brigades including 6 infantry and 1 armoured, and battalions include 4 engineers
Equipment: 149 tanks, 37 armoured cars and 123 APCs

Army Aviation

Fleet: 16 fixed and 33 rotary wing aircraft

Air Force

Personnel: 4,000
Organisation: 4 commands; combat (squadrons include 1 interceptor, 2 strike and 1 bomber), transport, training and helicopters

EGYPT

Navy

Personnel: 20,000
Fleet: 1 destroyer, 4 frigates, 8 submarines, 39 fast attack craft, 18 patrol craft, 6 mine hunters, 6 mine sweepers, 3 hovercraft mine layers and 3 MCMVs; Naval Aviation has a fleet of 27 helicopters

Army

Personnel: 300,000
Organisation: 2 field army HQs, 5 territorial areas with 4 armoured divisions, 5 mechanised infantry divisions and 3 infantry divisions
Equipment: 2,850 MBTs, 3,250 AIFVs and APCs and 112 armoured cars

Air Force

Personnel: 25,000
Organisation: combat forces consist of 5 fighter ground attack regiments, 9 fighter interceptor regiments and 2 recce AEW squadrons; in addition there are 3 transport regiments, 1 helicopter transport assault division and attack regiments

Air Defence Command

Personnel: 80,000
Organisation: 4 territorial air divisions

An Egyptian officer on UN duty

EL SALVADOR

Navy
Personnel: 1,300
Organisation: 1 infantry battalion and 1 special forces battalion
Fleet: 43 patrol craft and other light forces

Marines
Personnel: 600

Army
Personnel: 40,000
Organisation: 4 military zones are covered by brigades including 6 infantry and 1 artillery, totalling 37 battalions
Equipment: 5 MBTs, 10 armoured cars and 31 APCs

Air Force
Personnel: 2,200
Organisation: 3 commands, including combat command with 1 fighter bomber squadron

EQUATORIAL GUINEA

Navy
Personnel: 120
Fleet: 5 patrol craft

Army
Personnel: 1,400
Organisation: 2 infantry battalions
Equipment: 6 armoured cars

and 8 APCs

Air Force
Personnel: 120
Fleet: 5 aircraft

ETHIOPIA

Navy
Fleet: 2 frigates, 1 mine sweeper, 4 fast attack craft, 9 patrol craft and 8 landing craft

Army
Personnel: 22,500
Equipment: 395 MBTs, 90 armoured cars and 180 AIFVs and APCs

Air Force
Personnel: 3,500
Organisation: 42 combat aircraft , 12 transports making 1 squadron, 3 training squadrons and 46 helicopters
Note: all figures for Ethiopia must be considered doubtful

FIJI

Navy
Personnel: 280
Fleet: 27 patrol boats, 5 mine sweepers and 1 survey boat

Army
Personnel: 4,700
Organisation: 3 infantry battalions, 1 engineer company, 1 artillery battery

An ever-watchful Fijian soldier of the UN observation force reports back to headquarters

Below: *a Fijian Army cap badge*

and 1 special operations company
Equipment: includes 1 helicopter

FINLAND

Navy
Personnel: 2,500 including 1,300 conscripts
Fleet: 2 corvettes, 6 mine layers, 13 mine sweepers, 23 patrol craft and light forces, plus 7 landing craft

Army
Personnel: 27,300 including 21,600 conscripts
Organisation: 1 armoured brigade, 8 infantry training brigades and 1 field artillery brigade

Equipment: 138 tanks and 739 AIFVs and APCs

Air Force
Personnel: 3,000 including 1,500 conscripts
Organisation: 3 air defence wings, 3 fighter, 1 recce and 1 transport squadron

FRANCE

Navy
Personnel: 49,500 including 19,100 conscripts plus 2,500 marines
Fleet: 2 aircraft carriers, 1 cruiser, 15 destroyers, 23 frigates, 18 submarines, 15 mine hunters, 9 assault ships, plus other amphibious forces, light forces and support ships

Naval Aviation
Personnel: 12,000
Organisation: 3 strike, 1

Finnish para wings (other ranks)

interceptor, 1 AEW/ASW, 5 maritime recce, 1 recce, 3 ASW helicopter, 1 assault helicopter, and 2 SAR liaison squadrons

Army
Personnel: 261,000 including 178,000 conscripts
Organisation: 3 military defence regions with 8 active divisions shared between Rapid Reaction Force (FAR) with 1 air mobile division, 1 parachute division, 1 marine infantry division and 1 armoured division and the Armoured Mechanical Corps (CBM), with 4 armoured and mechanised divisions
Equipment: 1,500+ MBTs, 1,090 armoured cars and 4,610 MICVs and APCs

Above: *the badge of the Légionnaire 2e REP, France*

Below: *a French paratroop regimental badge*

Army Aviation
Personnel: 6,450
Organisation: 7 light groups
Fleet: 600 fixed and rotary wing aircraft

Air Force
Personnel: 92,000 including 34,000 conscripts
Organisation: 3 air regions are approximately covered by 3 corresponding air defence zones, established in 1993 and each containing 2 air defence sectors. Strategic Air Forces Command (FAS) is responsible for all air assets and the main nuclear mission. Tactical Air Force Command (FATAC) operates all other combat aircraft. The other 2 commands are Air Defence (CAFDA) and Military Transport (COTAM).

The 3 wings operated by FAS are No 91 Bomber Wing, with 2 squadrons, No 4 Fighter Bomber Wing with 3 squadrons, and No 93 Flight Refuelling Wing, with 3 squadrons. FATAC operates Fighter Wings Nos 2, 3, 5, 11, 12, 13 and 30 in addition to No 4 30 Fighter Squadron, No 7 Fighter Bomber Wing, No 33 Reconnaissance Wing and a tactical training centre

GABON

Navy
Personnel: 470
Fleet: 1 fast attack craft and 6 patrol craft; the coast guard has a fleet of 9 patrol craft

Army

Personnel: 2,200
Organisation: 1 presidential guard, 8 infantry companies, 1 paratroop commando company and 1 engineer company
Equipment: 40 armoured cars and 42 APCs

Air Force

Personnel: 600
Organisation: 1 fighter ground attack squadron, 1 maritime patrol unit, 14 helicopters and 7 transport liaison aircraft; the Presidential Guard Air Wing has a fleet of 1 helicopter and 11 fixed wing aircraft

GAMBIA, THE

Navy

Personnel: 50
Fleet: 4 patrol craft

Army

Personnel: 425
Organisation: 1 company
Equipment: 8 scout cars

Air Wing

Personnel: 25
Organisation: 1 transport squadron with 2 aircraft

GERMANY

Navy

Personnel: (at end 1994) 26,200 including conscripts

Panzergrenadier insignia of the former West Germany

Fleet: 6 destroyers, 10 frigates, 22 submarines, 40 fast attack craft, 74 mine warfare and amphibious forces and over 50 support and auxiliary ships

Naval Aviation

Organisation: 1 ASW, 3 fighter strike, 1 helicopter ASW, 1 helicopter anti-ship and 1 liaison squadron

Army

Personnel: (at end 1994) 255,400 including conscripts
Organisation: (currently) the 3 corps are comprised of 12 divisions (6 armoured, 4 armoured infantry, 1 airborne and 1 mountain infantry) and are made up of 38 brigades. Of

Fallschirmjäger insignia of the former West Germany

these, 17 are armoured, each with 3 tank battalions, 1 armoured infantry battalion and 1 armoured artillery battalion; 15 armoured infantry brigades, each with 1 tank battalion, 3 armoured infantry battalions and 1 armoured artillery battalion; in addition to 3 airborne brigades, 1 mountain brigade, 3 air defence regiments, 11 anti-aircraft regiments, 8 MLRS battalions and 3 Army Aviation commands

Equipment: 4,070 MBTs, 635 armoured recce, 4,224 AIFVs and APCs, 486 tank destroyers, and Army Aviation has 733 helicopters

Air Force

Personnel: (at end 1994) 89,000 including conscripts

Organisation: (under 'Plan 1994') 4 air divisions with 4 fighter wings (8 squadrons), 3 fighter bomber wings (10 squadrons), 1 recce ECR wing (2 squadrons), 3 transport wings (7 squadrons), 6 SAM wings (72 squadrons) and 1 SAM group (13 squadrons)

A combat dress shoulder patch of the German One Corps, 1958

GHANA

Navy

Personnel: 800

Fleet: 4 patrol boats

Army

Personnel: 4,300
Organisation: 2 command HQs, 2 infantry brigades, 1 recce battalion, 1 engineer battalion, 3 border troop battalions, 1 mortar battalion, 1 paratroop battalion and 1 commando company
Equipment: 58 armoured cars

Air Force

Personnel: 900
Organisation: 1 COIN light attack, 1 transport and 1 helicopter squadron

GREECE

Navy

Personnel: 19,500 including 11,000 conscripts serving for 19-23 months
Fleet: 12 destroyers, 6 frigates, 5 corvettes, 10 submarines, 2 mine layers, 14 mine sweepers, 10 torpedo boats and other light forces and amphibious forces; Naval Aviation has 14 helicopters

Army

Personnel: 118,000 including 100,000 conscripts
Organisation: 4 corps HQs, 2 division HQs (1 armoured, 1 mechanised) and 10 infantry divisions
Equipment: MBTs being increased to 1,155, 30 armoured cars, and AFVs being increased to about 2,500; in addition, Army Aviation has about 150 fixed and rotary wing aircraft

Air Force

Personnel: 18,000 including 14,000 conscripts serving for 17-21 months
Organisation: Hellenic Tactical Air Force (HTAF) and Hellenic Air Support Command (HASC) form the two operational commands, the HTAF having 6 wings (17 squadrons) and the HASC 3 transport and 3 helicopter squadrons

GUATEMALA

Navy

Personnel: 1,200
Fleet: coastal patrol craft

Marines

Personnel: 700

Army

Personnel: 40,000
Organisation: 22 military zones are covered; forces include 40 infantry battalions and 20 artillery batteries
Equipment: 10 MBTs, 5 armoured cars and 45 APCs

Air Force

Personnel: 1,300
Organisation: combat, training,

transport, helicopter and liaison commands

GUINEA

Coast Guard (navy)
Personnel: 400
Fleet: 11 patrol craft and 2 hydrofoils

Army
Personnel: 8,500
Organisation: 5 infantry, 1 armoured, 1 artillery, 1 engineer battalion, 1 para commando brigade and 1 air defence battalion
Equipment: 4 MBTs, 24 armoured cars and 40 APCs

Air Force
Personnel: 800
Organisation: 1 fighter ground attack, 1 transport, 1 training and 1 helicopter squadron

GUINEA-BISSAU

Navy
Personnel: 300
Fleet: 2 hydrofoils and 6 patrol boats

Army
Personnel: 4,500
Organisation: 1 armoured, 4 infantry, 1 artillery, 1 ranger battalion and 1 ranger unit
Equipment: 26 MBTs, 12 armoured cars and 49 APCs

Air Force
Personnel: 100
Organisation: 1 fighter squadron and 1 transport liaison unit

GUYANA

Army
Personnel: 1,500
Organisation: 6 battalions
Equipment: 4 APCs

Maritime Corps
Personnel: 200
Fleet: 5 patrol craft

Air Corps
Personnel: 300
Organisation: only 2 fixed and 2 rotary wing aircraft are operational

HAITI

Navy
Personnel: 340
Organisation: coast guard duties only operated
Fleet: 3 patrol craft and 9 armed launches

Army
Personnel: 7,000
Organisation: 9 military departments, including 1 infantry battalion
Equipment: 5 MBTs and 11 APCs

Air Force
Personnel: 300
Organisation: combat, transport, helicopter and training commands

HONDURAS

Navy
Personnel: 1,200
Fleet: 29 patrol craft and other light forces

Marines
Personnel: 600
Organisation: 1 battalion

Army
Personnel: 14,000
Organisation: 10 military zones covered; forces include 3 infantry brigades
Equipment: 15 tanks and 80 armoured cars

Air Force
Personnel: 1,800
Organisation: 4 commands include combat command, with 1 fighter bomber squadron

HUNGARY

Army
Personnel: 58,700 including 38,800 conscripts
Organisation: 3 corps HQs with 21 brigades of which 3 are armoured, 1 airborne battalion and 1 helicopter regiment

Equipment: 1,352 MBTs, of which nearly half are non-operational, 310 scout cars and 1,694 AIFVs and APCs. Army Aviation has 2 transport squadrons with 11 fixed wing aircraft and 4 helicopter squadrons with 118 helicopters

Air Force
Personnel: 18,300 including 12,900 conscripts
Organisation: 3 air regiments which include 6 fighter and 1 recce squadron

ICELAND

Defence Department
Personnel: 3,000
Equipment: 3 patrol vessels, 1 fixed and 2 rotary wing aircraft

INDIA

Navy
Personnel: 53,000 including 1,000 marines and 15,300 coast guard
Fleet: 2 aircraft carriers, 5 destroyers, 13 frigates, 19 submarines, 20 corvettes, 8 FACs, 37 patrol craft, 22 mine sweepers and other amphibious and auxiliary forces

Naval Aviation
Personnel: 2,000
Organisation: 2 attack, 1 strike, 2 maritime recce, 2 anti-ship, 4

coast guard and 6 ASW squadrons, together with light transport, liaison and training aircraft

Army
Personnel: 1,100,000
Organisation: 5 regional HQs, 10 corps HQs, 2 armoured, 1 mechanised, 20 infantry, 11 mountain and 1 air mobile divisions, 19 various

Indian Army

independent brigades, 3 artillery brigades, 5 air defence brigades, 5 engineer brigades, 1 airborne regiment and 1 para commando regiment
Equipment: 3,650 MBTs, 600 MICVs and APCs; Army Aviation comprises 13 observation/liaison and 2 attack squadrons plus about 400 helicopters

Air Force
Personnel: 115,000
Organisation: 13 fighter interceptor and fighter ground attack, 19 air defence, 3 recce, 9 helicopter liaison, 4 helicopter transport, 4 helicopter attack and 13 transport squadrons, plus trainer aircraft

INDONESIA

Navy
Personnel: 28,000
Fleet: 17 frigates, 16 corvettes, 2 submarines, 5 missile FACs, 12 FACs, 4 SAR patrol boats, 7 patrol boats, 12 patrol hydrofoils, 2 mine hunters, 13 mine sweepers and other assorted amphibious vessels

Naval Aviation
Personnel: 1,000
Organisation: 1 maritime recce squadron, 1 transport liaison

unit, 1 helicopter unit and 1 SAR unit

Marines
Personnel: 12,000
Equipment: 30 light tanks and 59 APCs

Army
Personnel: 220,000
Organisation: 3 divisional HQs, 1 armoured cavalry brigade, 4 infantry, 2 airborne and 1 para commando brigade, 2 artillery regiments, 2 engineer battalions, 10 regional commands with 60 independent infantry battalions, 10 independent armoured battalions, 8 independent artillery battalions and 9 independent air defence battalions. There is also a Special Warfare Command, with 1 special commando force and 1 counter terrorist unit
Equipment: 156 MBTs, 161 armoured cars and 610 APCs; Army Aviation has a fleet of 88 helicopters, together with fixed wing transport liaison aircraft

Air Force
Personnel: 25,000
Organisation: 2 fighter ground attack, 2 fighter attack, 1 COIN, 1 MR recce, 4 transport, 3 helicopter and 2 Air Force Academy squadrons

IRAN

Navy
Personnel: 15,000 including Marines
Fleet: 3 destroyers, 3 frigates, 2 corvettes, 2 submarines, 3 mine sweepers and light forces, landing craft and other amphibious forces; Naval Aviation has a fleet of over 50 helicopters

Army
Personnel: 350,000
Organisation: 3 army HQs with 10 divisions
Equipment: about 700 MTBs, 720 AIFVs and APCs; Army Aviation has a fleet of about 80 fixed and 375 rotary wing aircraft

Air Force
Personnel: 35,000
Organisation: 8 fighter strike and 6 transport squadrons, plus maritime patrol, trainers and helicopters

IRAQ

Navy
Personnel: 5,000 including 3,000 conscripts
Fleet: 1 non-operational frigate, 4 patrol craft, 6 torpedo boats and 4 mine sweepers, together with miscellaneous craft

An Iraqi Army Armoured Division badge

Army
Personnel: 300,000
Organisation: 1 armoured division, 1 mechanised division, 18 infantry divisions, 2 special forces brigades and 13 presidential guard battalions (these figures may well be much higher)
Equipment: about 2,000 MBTs, 1,000 armoured cars and 2,000 AIFVs and APCs; Army Aviation operates a helicopter fleet

Air Force
Personnel: 30,000
Organisation: unclear, but probably about 250 surviving fixed wing aircraft exist, together with a helicopter fleet of 11 squadrons

IRELAND (EIRE)

Naval Service (navy)
Personnel: 931
Fleet: 7 patrol craft

Army
Personnel: 11,000
Organisation: 11 infantry battalions including 1 armoured and 4 recce squadrons

Below: *an arm badge of the Irish Southern Command*

Equipment: 14 light tanks, 51 armoured cars and 70 APCs

Air Corps (air force)
Personnel: 900
Organisation: combat command comprises 1 COIN squadron with 1 training unit and 1 liaison unit

ISRAEL

Navy
Personnel: 9,000 including 3,000 conscripts serving for 24 months (women) and 36 months (men)
Fleet: 3 submarines, 3 corvettes, 20 missile fast attack craft, 3 missile hydrofoils, 30 patrol craft and other amphibious forces; Naval Aviation operates 2 shipborne helicopters and there is 1 Special Forces unit with a frogman squadron

Army
Personnel: 110,000 including 90,000 men and women conscripts
Organisation: armoured divisions comprise mechanised infantry brigades, infantry brigades, a paratroop brigade, territorial brigades with 3 division HQs for border defence, and a special operations battalion

Golani Infantry Brigade, Israeli Army

Israeli Defence Forces Airborne Brigade

Equipment: 1,265 MTBs and 5,000 APCs

Air Force
Personnel: 27,000 including 18,000 conscripts
Organisation: 19 fighter ground attack and interceptor squadrons make up the combat force, together with over 250 helicopters

ITALY

Navy
Personnel: 38,680 including 13,500 conscripts

Fleet: 1 aircraft carrier (V/STOL), 1 helicopter carrier, 4 destroyers, 16 frigates, 12 corvettes, 10 submarines, 6 missile hydrofoils, 8 patrol vessels, 17 mine hunters, 2 mine sweepers, amphibious forces and service forces

Naval Aviation
Personnel: 1,500
Organisation: 1 fixed and 2 rotary wing ASW squadrons

Marines
Personnel: 1,500
Organisation: 1 regiment and 1 special operations command

Army
Personnel: 174,000 including

The badge of the Folgore Brigade, Italy

90,000 conscripts
Organisation: comprises 3 main groups; ready intervention forces, 'second use' forces and reserve forces. The ready intervention forces are kept in permanent combat ready status, and are based on 3 brigades manned entirely by professionals
Equipment: 1,220 MBTs and over 5,000 APCs

Army Aviation
Organisation: 1 fixed and 20 rotary wing units
Fleet: 50 fixed and 350 rotary wing aircraft

Air Force
Personnel: 63,000 including 20,000 conscripts
Organisation: combat command comprises 6 fighter, 3 all weather strike and 5 light attack recce training squadrons

JAMAICA

Army
Personnel: 2,800
Organisation: 2 infantry battalions plus 1 support battalion
Equipment: 15 APCs

Coast Guard
Personnel: 180
Fleet: 12 patrol craft

A Jamaica Defence Forces Badge

Air Wing
Personnel: 150
Fleet: 16 aircraft

JAPAN

Maritime Self Defence Force (navy)
Personnel: 32,000
Fleet: 39 destroyers, 20 frigates, 18 submarines, 6 mine layers, 30 mine sweepers, 2 hydrofoil FACs, 15 patrol craft and numerous other amphibious forces and small craft including 50 small landing craft

Maritime Safety Agency (coast guard)
Personnel: 12,000
Fleet: 52 cutters, 80 patrol boats and 180 coastal patrol boats

Naval Aviation
Personnel: 11,000
Organisation: 16 maritime patrol and ASW, 1 transport, 9 helicopter ASW, 1 helicopter mine countermeasures, 3 SAR and 6 training utility squadrons

Ground Self Defence Force (army)
Personnel: 150,000

Above: *the Japanese Airborne Ranger insignia*

Organisation: 5 army HQs, 12 infantry and 1 armoured divisions, 2 composite, 1 airborne, 1 helicopter, 1 artillery and 5 engineer brigades, 8 SAM groups plus 2 artillery groups
Equipment: 1,215 MBTs and 980 APCs; Army Aviation has a fleet of 6 liaison and 24 helicopter squadrons

Air Self Defence Force (air force)
Personnel: 44,500
Organisation: 5 major commands cover air defence, air support, transport, training and supplies, and comprise 12 fighter, 3 fighter ground attack, 1 recce, 3 transport, 2 AEW and 1 ELINT EW squadron, 1 SAR air rescue wing, 8 training squadrons and 1 liaison flight

JORDAN

Coast Guard (navy)
Personnel: 300
Fleet: 18 patrol craft

Army
Personnel: 75,000
Organisation: 4 divisional HQs (2 armoured, 2 mechanised), 5 armoured brigades, 6 mechanised brigades, 1 royal guard brigade, 1 special forces (airborne) brigade, 1 special

operations battalion, 16 artillery battalions and 1 anti-aircraft brigade
Equipment: 3,548 MTBs, of which 2,690 are stored, and 1,590 AFVs

Air Force
Personnel: 11,000
Organisation: 2 interceptor, 4 fighter ground attack, 2 transport, 2 helicopter combat and 4 helicopter transport liaison squadrons

KENYA

Navy
Personnel: 1,350
Fleet: 6 fast attack craft and 4 patrol craft

Kenyan peacekeeping forces from the para commando battalion were attached to the UN

43

Army

Personnel: 19,000
Organisation: 1 armoured, 2 infantry, 1 artillery, 1 engineer brigade, 1 air cavalry, 1 support, 1 transport, 1 para commando and 1 anti-aircraft battalion
Equipment: 80 MBTs, 82 armoured cars and 38 APCs

Air Force

Personnel: 2,500
Organisation: 1 fighter ground attack, 1 COIN light attack, 2 transport and 20 trainers and 50 helicopters

KUWAIT

Navy

Personnel: 1,000
Fleet: 6 missile FACs, 6 patrol craft, and fast strike craft

Army

Personnel: 25,000
Organisation: 1 mechanised division (2 brigades), 1 armoured division (2 brigades) and 1 special forces battalion
Equipment: 330 + MBTs and about 200 APCs; Kuwait is still in the process of rearming and reorganisation

Air Force

Organisation: no structure has yet been established, but Kuwait does now have the aircraft returned from Iraq, together with new fighters and trainers plus helicopters

LAOS

Army

Personnel: 50,000
Organisation: 4 regional HQs, 5 infantry divisions, 7 independent infantry regiments, 2 engineer regiments, 1 construction regiment, 1 armoured battalion and 15 artillery battalions, together with special forces and a raiders regiment
Equipment: 55 MBTs, 25 armoured cars and 100 APCs; Army Aviation has a fleet of 4 fixed wing aircraft, and the navy (riverine) section of the Army a personnel strength of 600 and a fleet of 40 patrol craft and launches

Air Force

Personnel: 2,000
Organisation: 2 fighter ground attack squadrons, 2 transport and 1 helicopter squadron and 14 trainers

LEBANON, THE

Navy

Personnel: 400
Fleet: 10 patrol craft and 2 landing craft

The insignia of the 1983 Multinational Force stationed in Beirut, the Lebanon

Army
Personnel: up to 40,000
Organisation: normally 11 infantry brigades
Equipment: 166 MBTs, 60 armoured cars and about 300 APCs

Air Force
Personnel: 800
Organisation: 1 FGA, 1 transport and 1 helicopter squadron

LIBYA

Navy
Personnel: 7,800 including coast guard
Fleet: 3 frigates, 7 corvettes, 12 submarines, 25 fast attack craft, 21 patrol craft, 8 mine sweepers and other amphibious forces; Naval Aviation has a fleet of 26 helicopters

Army
Personnel: 51,000
Organisation: 11 armoured brigades, 11 mechanised infantry brigades, 5 infantry brigades, 1 national guard brigade, 40 independent armoured battalions, 48 independent mechanised infantry battalions, 12 airborne battalions, 4 ranger battalions, 2 artillery regiments and 6 SSM brigades
Equipment: 635 MBTs, 950

Beret para wings badge of the Libyan Army

45

armoured cars, 1,533 AIFVs and APCs; Army Aviation has a fleet of 21 helicopters

Air Force
Personnel: 18,000
Organisation: 10 fighter, 1 strike, 1 recce, 2 COIN, 2 transport and 4 helicopter squadrons

LUXEMBOURG

Army
Personnel: 750
Organisation: 1 light infantry battalion
Equipment: 5 APCs

MADAGASCAR

Navy
Personnel: 600 including 1 marine company
Fleet: 7 patrol boats

Army
Personnel: 20,000
Organisation: 2 infantry battalions, 1 engineer, 1 signals and 1 service regiment, 7 construction regiments and 1 commando company
Equipment: 10 MBTs, 44 armoured cars and 75 APCs

Air Force
Personnel: 500
Organisation: 1 fighter ground

attack and 1 transport liaison squadron plus 6 helicopters

MALAWI

Army
Personnel: 9,500
Organisation: 3 infantry battalions, 1 support battalion and 1 commando company
Equipment: 38 armoured cars
Note: there is a naval detachment of 200 personnel which is part of the army, with a fleet of 2 patrol boats plus other small craft. The Army Air Wing has a fleet of 6 transports and 8 helicopters

MALAYSIA

Navy
Personnel: 12,300
Fleet: 6 frigates, 14 FACs and 40 patrol craft, together with some mine warfare vessels and other amphibious forces; the naval air wing has a fleet of 12 helicopters

Army
Personnel: 97,000
Organisation: 1 corps, 4 divisional HQs, and 9 infantry brigades with a total of 36 infantry battalions, 4 armoured regiments, 5 field artillery regiments, 2 anti-aircraft artillery batteries, 5 signal and 5 engineer

The insignia of the Malaysian Riot Control Unit

regiments, and a special service regiment comprised of 4 battalions and 1 airborne ranger battalion
Equipment: 78 light tanks, 482 armoured cars and 750 APCs

Air Force
Personnel: 12,000
Organisation: 2 aircraft commands with 1 fighter, 3 fighter ground attack, 1 recce, 1 COIN, 1 MR, 5 transport, 4 liaison and 3 training squadrons

MALI

Navy
Personnel: 70
Fleet: 3 river patrol boats

Army
Personnel: 7,000

Organisation: 2 armoured, 4 infantry, 1 paratroop special forces, 2 artillery and 1 engineer battalions; 2 commando companies, 2 anti-aircraft artillery companies and 1 SAM battery
Equipment: 36 MBTs, 20 armoured cars and 34 APCs

Air Force
Personnel: 450
Organisation: 1 fighter ground attack squadron, 8 transport aircraft, 3 helicopters and 9 trainers

MALTA

Army
Personnel: 910
Organisation: 1 task force comprised of 1 infantry and 1 engineer battalion, 1 airport company and 1 security company

Maritime Force
Fleet: 3 mine sweepers, 4 patrol craft and 3 customs launches

Army Aviation
Fleet: 11 helicopters

MAURITANIA

Navy
Personnel: 300
Fleet: 12 patrol craft

Army

Personnel: 8,600
Organisation: 7 infantry battalions, 2 armoured car squadrons, 1 para commando battalion, 2 camel corps battalions, 1 recce squadron, 2 artillery batteries, 1 engineer company, and 4 anti-aircraft batteries
Equipment: 88 armoured cars; Army Aviation has a fleet of 2 transports

Air Force

Personnel: 850
Organisation: 14 fixed wing transport liaison aircraft

MEXICO

Navy

Personnel: 35,000
Fleet: 3 destroyers, 5 frigates, 41 corvettes and 57 patrol craft

Marines

Personnel: 3,800
Organisation: 1 brigade, 1 presidential guard battalion and 32 security companies

Naval Air Arm

Personnel: 500
Organisation: 32 fixed and 22 rotary wing aircraft

Army

Personnel: 127,000 including 60,000 conscripts

Organisation: includes 36 independent local garrisons comprising 80 infantry battalions, 20 cavalry regiments, 3 artillery regiments, 1 armoured battalion and 1 mechanised infantry battalion
Equipment: 20 tanks, 145 APCs and 165 armoured cars

Air Force

Personnel: 8,000
Organisation: combat command (includes 1 fighter squadron), transport, training and helicopter commands

MOÇAMBIQUE

Navy

Personnel: 1,000
Fleet: 15 light and patrol forces craft

Army

Personnel: 37,000
Organisation: 10 regional HQs, 1 armoured brigade, 7 infantry brigades, 1 light infantry brigade, independent artillery battalions and 1 commando battalion
Equipment: 92 MBTs, 28 armoured cars and 180 APCs

Air Force

Personnel: 4,000
Organisation: 3 fighter ground attack and 1 transport

squadron plus 11 helicopters and 20 trainers

MONGOLIA

Army
Personnel: 15,000 plus conscripts serving for 24 months
Organisation: 3 infantry divisions, 2 SAM battalions, 1 construction brigade and 1 special forces unit
Equipment: 600 MBTs, 730 MICVs and APCs

Air Force Battle Order
Personnel: 1,000 plus conscripts serving for 24 months
Organisation: 1 fighter regiment operating as a squadron, 2 transport, 1 trainer and 3 helicopter squadrons

MOROCCO

Navy
Personnel: 6,500 including 1,500 marines and coast guard service
Fleet: 1 frigate, 6 fast attack craft, 21 patrol boats and other amphibious forces

Army
Personnel: 125,000
Organisation: 3 regional HQs with 1 mechanised infantry brigade (5 regiments), 2 motorised infantry brigades (14 regiments), 1 light infantry brigade, 2 paratroop brigades, 9 independent armoured squadrons, 35 independent infantry battalions and 12 other battalions and 11 artillery groups
Equipment: 429 MBTs, 336 armoured cars and 705 APCs

Air Force
Personnel: 13,000
Organisation: 1 fighter, 3 fighter bomber, 2 COIN and 1 transport squadron plus coastal patrol, trainers and helicopters

MYANMAR (UNION OF)

Navy
Personnel: 12,000 including 800 marines
Fleet: 4 corvettes, 25 patrol boats, 35 river patrol craft, 12 river gunboats and 15 landing craft; the naval air arm operates 3 squadrons

Army
Personnel: 250,000
Organisation: 10 regional HQs, 8 light infantry divisions, 2 armoured battalions, 27 independent infantry battalions, 4 artillery battalions, 1 anti-aircraft battery, 85 infantry battalions, 1 special forces airborne battalion and 5 commando

units
Equipment: 25 light tanks and 85 armoured cars

Air Force
Personnel: 9,000
Organisation: 2 COIN, 3 transport, 4 helicopter, 1 liaison and 2 further squadrons; trainer, transport aircraft and helicopters

NAMIBIA

Army
Personnel: 8,000
Organisation: 1 presidential guard battalion, 4 motorised infantry battalions, 1 artillery battalion and 1 anti-aircraft battalion
Equipment: 18 APCs

NEPAL

Army
Personnel: 35,000
Organisation: 2 divisional HQs, 5 infantry brigades, 1 palace guard brigade, 1 paratroop battalion, 1 artillery regiment, 1 engineer regiment, 1 airborne battalion and 1 recce unit
Equipment: 25 armoured cars; Army Aviation has a fleet of 4 fixed and 12 rotary wing aircraft

Right: *a Nepalese soldier on UN duty*

NETHERLANDS, THE

Navy
Personnel: 10,773 including 1,563 conscripts
Fleet: 12 frigates, 6 submarines, 15 mine hunters and 9 mine sweepers, plus combat support ships and miscellaneous craft

Naval Aviation
Personnel: 1,600
Organisation: 13 fixed and 22 rotary wing aircraft

Marines
Personnel: 2,600
Organisation: 2 amphibious combat groups, 1 mountain Arctic warfare company, 1 amphibious commando group and 1 special boat section

The Royal Netherlands Marine Corps

Army

Personnel: in the process of being reduced to 40,000 by 1995, and 36,000 by 1998
Organisation: 1 (NL) Corps is assigned to NATO and is organised as 2 divisional HQs, 2 armoured brigades (being reduced to 1), 1 air mobile brigade, 4 mechanised infantry brigades, 4 recce battalions, 3 helicopter squadrons, 5 anti-aircraft battalions and 1 commando command. By 1998, these will be reduced to 4 active brigades
Equipment: 743 MBTs, 2,777 AIVFs and APCs (this will alter radically as manpower is reduced and reorganised in the second half of the 1990s)

Air Force

Personnel: 15,378 including 3,384 conscripts
Organisation: Tactical Air

Command comprises 8 fighter bomber, 1 recce and 1 MR squadron based in the Dutch Antilles. Logistic and Training Command comprises 1 transport and 2 training squadrons and 1 SAR helicopter flight

NEW ZEALAND

Navy

Personnel: 2,494
Fleet: 4 frigates, 3 survey vessels, 4 patrol craft and miscellaneous craft; Naval

An airman wears the Royal New Zealand Air Force shoulder patch during the Triad '84 exercise; Whenuapai Air Base, New Zealand

Aviation has a fleet of 7 helicopters

Army

Personnel: 5,000
Organisation: an integrated expansion force (IEF) and a ready reaction force; there are 2 infantry battalions
Equipment: 26 MBTs and 78 APCs

Air Force

Personnel: 790
Organisation: 1 fighter ground attack, 1 OCU recce, 1 advance pilot training, 1 maritime patrol and 3 transport squadrons

The insignia of the New Zealand Special Air Service

NICARAGUA

Navy

Personnel: 1,000
Fleet: 9 torpedo boats, plus patrol craft, other light forces and 7 mine sweepers

Army

Personnel: 14,000
Organisation: 7 military regions are covered; battalions include 4 armoured and 4 mechanised infantry
Equipment: 175 tanks, 145 APCs and 70 armoured cars

Air Force

Personnel: 2,000
Organisation: combat, transport, helicopter and training commands

NIGER

Army

Personnel: 3,150
Organisation: 6 infantry companies, 2 armoured recce squadrons, 1 engineer company and 1 para commando company
Equipment: 46 armoured cars and 14 APCS

Air Force

Personnel: 140
Organisation: 12 fixed wing aircraft

NIGERIA

Navy

Personnel: 10,000
Fleet: 2 frigates, 3 corvettes, 6 FACs, 14 patrol craft, 2 mine hunters and other miscellaneous and auxiliary vessels. The coast guard

A Nigerian Army representative, seconded to the UN

operates a fleet of 35 patrol craft, 50 small launches and 5 hovercraft

Army
Personnel: 70,000
Organisation: 1 armoured, 2 mechanised and 1 combined arms divisions; 1 paratroop brigade, 4 artillery regiments, 4 engineer battalions, 1 guards battalion and 1 commando battalion
Equipment: 222 MBTs, 174 armoured cars and 336 APCs

Air Force
Personnel: 9,500
Organisation: 3 fighter ground attack, 2 COIN training, 2 transport, 1 liaison, 1 helicopter and 3 training squadrons

NORTH KOREA (DPRK)

Navy
Personnel: 41,500
Fleet: 3 frigates, 25 submarines, 45 midget submarines, 39 FACs, 237 torpedo boats, 140 patrol craft and various other amphibious forces including 58 hovercraft

Army
Personnel: 930,000 including 70,000 commando force
Organisation: 17 corps HQs, 2 armoured, 31 infantry and 5 mechanised divisions, 6 independent armoured brigades, 4 artillery brigades, 20 independent artillery regiments, 2 SAM divisions, 5 SSM regiments, 5 airborne battalions and 1 special forces corps
Equipment: 3,625 MBTs, 140 armoured cars and 2,000+ APCs

Air Force
Personnel: 70,000
Organisation: 3 light bomber, 11 FGA, 12 interceptor, 1 recce, 3 transport, 14 helicopter and 7 training squadrons

NORWAY

Navy
Organisation: naval defence is divided into 8 naval districts

defended by the Royal Norwegian Navy and the Coastal Artillery

Royal Norwegian Navy
Personnel: 7,500
Fleet: 5 frigates, 12 submarines, 30 missile fast attack craft, mine warfare forces and amphibious forces
Coastal Artillery
Personnel: 2,000
Organisation: 32 artillery batteries

Army
Personnel: 20,000 including 15,000 conscripts serving for 12 months

A Norwegian UN soldier on duty in the Lebanon

Organisation: 5 regional commands and 15 territorial commands
Equipment: 210 tanks, 68 AIFVs and APCs and 97 tank destroyers

Air Force
Personnel: 9,500 including 4,600 conscripts
Organisation: 4 main air stations, with 10 smaller stations and 6 radar stations. There are 4 fighter ground attack, 1 ASW maritime patrol, 2 transport and 2 helicopter squadrons (1 SAR and 1 coast guard)

OMAN

Navy
Personnel: 3,400
Fleet: 1 corvette, 8 FACS, 4 patrol craft, and other amphibious vessels; the coast guard has 20 patrol craft

Army
Personnel: 21,000
Organisation: 2 brigade HQs with 8 infantry and 2 artillery regiments; in addition there is 1 regiment each for recce, field engineers and paratroops; most regiments are battalion size
Equipment: 109 MBTs, 38 armoured cars, and APCs

54

PAKISTAN

The Omani Army cap badge

Air Force
Personnel: 5,000
Organisation: 2 fighter ground attack squadrons which also cover reconnaissance, 1 COIN, 3 transport and 2 helicopter squadrons

The Sultan's Special Forces, Oman

Navy
Personnel: 18,500 including Naval Air Wing and Special Service Group
Fleet: 4 destroyers, 10 frigates, 9 submarines, 16 FACs, 5 FAC hydrofoils, 1 mine hunter and 3 mine sweepers; Naval Aviation operates 1 maritime recce and 1 helicopter squadron

Army
Personnel: 500,000
Organisation: 2 armoured divisions, 19 infantry divisions, 6 independent armoured brigades, 6 independent infantry brigades, 4 air defence brigades, 9 artillery brigades, 3 armoured recce regiments, 1 special services group of 3 battalions and 1 counter terrorist company
Equipment: 2,600+ MBTs, 100 armoured cars and 850 APCs; Army Aviation operates 4 helicopter and 1 liaison squadrons

Air Force
Personnel: 30,000
Organisation: 8 fighter interceptor, 10 fighter ground attack, 1 recce, 2 transport, 4 trainer and 2 helicopter squadrons and liaison aircraft

A Pakistani Army officer on UN duty

PANAMA

National Maritime Service (navy)
Personnel: 300
Organisation: coast guard duties only
Fleet: 17 craft in total

National Police
Personnel: 11,200
Organisation: Canal defence force and border guards
Equipment: 15 AFVs and 16 APCs

Air Force
Personnel: 400
Organisation: 37 fixed and rotary wing aircraft

PAPUA NEW GUINEA

Navy
Personnel: 420
Fleet: 5 patrol craft and 2 landing craft; the air arm comprises 6 aircraft for coastal surveillance

Army
Personnel: 2,862
Organisation: 2 infantry battalions, 1 engineer battalion, 1 signal squadron and 1 special operations company

Air Force
Personnel: 118
Fleet: 7 fixed and 4 rotary wing aircraft

PARAGUAY

Navy
Personnel: 3,000
Organisation: river guard duties
Fleet: 25 craft, including gunboats and patrol boats

Naval Aviation
Fleet: 19 fixed and rotary wing aircraft

Marines
Personnel: 500
Organisation: 1 marine and 1 commando battalion

Army
Personnel: 12,000
Organisation: 8 infantry divisions and 1 cavalry division
Equipment: 25 tanks and 64 APCs

Air Force
Personnel: 1,000
Organisation: combat, transport, training and helicopter commands

PERU

Navy
Personnel: 20,000 including conscripts
Fleet: 2 cruisers, 6 destroyers, 4 frigates, 6 corvettes, 9 submarines and light forces including river gunboats and patrol craft

Naval Air Arm
Fleet: 25 fixed and 28 rotary wing aircraft

Marines
Personnel: 5,400 including Naval Air Arm
Organisation: 1 brigade

Army
Personnel: 75,000 including 50,000 conscripts
Organisation: 5 military regions
Equipment: 430 tanks, over 600 APCs and other AFVs

Army Aviation
Fleet: 76 fixed and rotary wing aircraft

Air Force
Personnel: 15,000
Organisation: combat, transport, trainer and helicopter (with 86 helicopters) commands

PHILIPPINES, THE

Navy
Personnel: 12,000
Fleet: 5 frigates, 10 corvettes, 20 patrol vessels, and other amphibious forces; Naval Aviation operates a fleet of 13 fixed and 11 rotary wing

aircraft

Marines
Personnel: 9,000
Organisation: 3 brigades
Equipment: 85 LVTPs

Coast Guard
Personnel: 2,000
Fleet: 65 patrol craft

Army
Personnel: 72,000
Organisation: 8 light infantry divisions, 1 scout ranger regiment, 1 special forces group, 3 engineer brigades, 1 light armoured brigade, 1 construction battalion and 1 special forces brigade
Equipment: 28 tanks, 161 APCs and 62 AIFVs; Army Aviation operates as 1 battalion

Air Force
Personnel: 15,361
Organisation: 1 interceptor, 2 COIN, 1 MP, 3 transport and 6 helicopter squadrons (1 transport wing), 1 SAR helicopter, 1 helicopter combat and 2 trainer squadrons plus 1 presidential aircraft wing

POLAND

Navy
Personnel: 19,300 including Naval Aviation and 11,600

The 6th Pomorska Airborne Brigade, Poland

conscripts
Fleet: 1 destroyer, 3 submarines, 5 corvettes, 8 missile fast attack craft, 28 mine sweepers and amphibious forces and transports; Naval Aviation has 2 helicopter squadrons comprising 22 helicopters

Army
Personnel: 162,130 including 127,500 conscripts
Organisation: 3 military districts, each with army HQ and comprising 11 mechanised divisions, 1 airborne brigade, 1 coastal defence brigade, 4 artillery brigades, 4 engineer brigades, 3 anti-tank artillery regiments, 3 anti-aircraft artillery regiments and 3 artillery rocket regiments

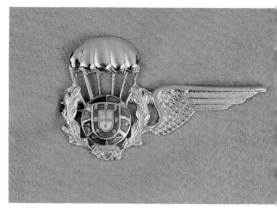

The 7th Polish Naval Assault Division

Equipment: 2,850 MBTs, 2,396 AIFVs and APCs

Air Force
Personnel: 82,200 including 52,000 conscripts
Organisation: the Air and Air Defence Force (AADF) is divided into 4 corps, with 4 air defence corps and 2 fighter bomber divisions, 8 fighter regiments, 3 fighter bomber regiments, 3 recce regiments, 1 tactical recce regiment, 2 transport regiments, 2 combat helicopter regiments and 1 transport helicopter regiment

PORTUGAL

Navy
Personnel: 12,500 including 5,000 conscripts

Portuguese para wings

Fleet: 17 frigates and 3 submarines, plus light and patrol forces; Naval Aviation has a fleet of 5 helicopters

Marines
Personnel: 2,500
Organisation: 3 brigades

Army
Personnel: 33,000 including 24,000 conscripts
Organisation: 6 regional commands, 1 light infantry task force, 3 infantry brigades, 1 combined arms brigade, 3 cavalry regiments, 1 special forces (airborne) brigade and 2 engineer regiments
Equipment: 112 MBTs, 100 armoured cars and 309 APCs

Air Force
Personnel: 13,500 including 2,500

paratroops and 4,500 conscripts serving for 18-20 months
Organisation: combat command has 2 attack, 2 fighter bomber and 1 MP squadron. There are 6 transport squadrons under transport command. Helicopter command comprises 4 squadrons in addition to light transport, liaison and trainer forces

QATAR

Navy
Personnel: 700
Fleet: 3 fast attack craft and 42 patrol craft

Army
Personnel: 6,000
Organisation: 1 tank battalion, 2 armoured car regiments, 1 guard regiment, 3 mechanised infantry battalions and 1 artillery battalion
Equipment: 24 MBTs, 85 armoured cars, 113 AIFVs and APCs

Air Force
Personnel: 300
Organisation: 2 fighter ground attack and 1 transport squadron and 34 helicopters

ROMANIA

Navy
Personnel: 19,000 including 10,000 conscripts
Fleet: 1 destroyer, 4 frigates, 1 submarine, 1 corvette, 19 patrol boats, 42 torpedo boats, 1 fast attack craft, 2 mine layers and 16 mine sweepers plus the Danube flotilla of small patrol craft and vedettes

Army
Personnel: 161,000 including 105,000 conscripts
Organisation: 4 commands, 2 tank divisions, 7 motorised divisions and a total of 15 brigades plus 6 anti-tank regiments, 5 air defence regiments and an airborne battalion
Equipment: 2,816 MBTs, 139 recce cars and 2,731 APCs

Air Force
Personnel: 20,000 including 10,000 conscripts
Organisation: combat command comprises 19 fighter, 7 fighter ground attack and 2 recce squadrons. There is a transport command of 1 regiment, helicopter command of 2 transport liaison regiments and 2 attack squadrons plus trainers

RWANDA

This was the situation prior to the civil war:

Personnel: 6,1000 including 1,000 conscripts
Fleet: 3 submarines, 9 FACs, 4 patrol boats, 3 patrol catamarans, 4 mine hunters, 4 mine sweepers and other auxiliary vessels

Marines
Personnel: 900
Organisation: 2 battalions

Army
Personnel: 50,000 including 32,000 conscripts
Organisation: 1 corps HQ plus 2 divisional HQs, 1 armoured division, 2 mechanised divisions, 1 parachute brigade, 2 field artillery regiments, 2 anti-aircraft regiments, 3 engineer regiments, 1 signal regiment, 3 signal squadrons and 1 special recce unit
Equipment: 250 MBTs, 2,000 armoured cars, 50 tank destroyers and 2,700 APCs

Air Force
Personnel: 16,000 including 2,000 conscripts
Organisation: 4 fighter ground attack and 1 maritime patrol squadron, plus 132 helicopters, 28 transport, 4 tankers and 330 trainers

SAUDI ARABIA

Navy
Personnel: 10,800 including 1,200 marines
Fleet: 4 frigates, 4 corvettes, 9 missile and 3 torpedo FACs, 17 patrol craft, 7 mine hunters, and other light forces, amphibious forces and auxiliaries; the coast guard has 83 patrol craft and 24 hovercraft, and Naval Aviation a fleet of 54 helicopters

Army
Personnel: 45,000
Organisation: 4 mechanised division HQs, with 2 armoured, 4 mechanised, 1 infantry and 1 airborne brigades, 5 artillery and 6 anti-aircraft regiments. The army is currently expanding from this strength, to 150,000 men in 8 divisions, with appropriate increases in equipment
Equipment: 950 MBTs, 200 tank destroyers, 700 armoured cars, 1,900 AIFVs and APCs; Army Aviation has a fleet of 28 helicopters

Air Force
Personnel: 18,000
Organisation: 2 strike, 6 fighter bomber, 4 interceptor, 2 COIN squadrons which also act as trainers and 1 recce squadron,

Para wings of Saudi Arabia

A Singapore Army arm patch

3 operational conversion units and 7 AEW aircraft, 16 tankers, 3 transport and 2 helicopter squadrons.

Air Defence Force
This is a separate force, responsible for all mobile and fixed air defence assets

National Guard
Organisation: 2 mechanised brigades and 2 special forces groups
Equipment: 500 + APCs

SINGAPORE

Navy
Personnel: 4,500
Organisation: fleet, coastal command and naval logistic command

Fleet: 6 corvettes, 12 FACs, 1 mine sweeper and other amphibious vessels; coastal command has 24 patrol craft and the marines a further 35 small patrol craft and launches

Army
Personnel: 45,000 including 30,000 conscripts serving for between 24 and 30 months, dependent upon rank
Organisation: 5 divisional HQs, 3 combined arms divisions, 1 air mobile brigade, 1 artillery brigade, 2 commando battalions, 6 engineer battalions and 3 signal battalions
Equipment: 333 tanks and 1,416 APCs

Air Force

Personnel: 6,000
Organisation: 2 fighter, 4 fighter ground attack, 1 fighter recce and 2 transport squadrons, 1 liaison unit, 1 AEW unit, 3 helicopter and 2 trainer squadrons

SOUTH KOREA (ROK)

Navy

Personnel: 35,000 including 20,000 conscripts
Fleet: 9 destroyers, 15 frigates, 26 corvettes, 100 FACs and patrol forces, 11 submarines (7 midget), 8 mine sweepers, 3 mine countermeasures and 32 landing ships; Naval Aviation operates 2 ASW, 1 maritime patrol and 2 liaison squadrons

Marine Raider para wings, South Korea

Marine Corps

Personnel: 25,000
Organisation: 2 infantry divisions and 1 infantry brigade
Equipment: 40 MBTs and 100 APCs

Army

Personnel: 550,000
Organisation: 3 army groups, 11 corps HQs with 2 mechanised, 19 infantry, 9 airborne, 1 Army Aviation, 3 independent infantry, 3 independent mechanised, 7 special forces and 2 air defence brigades, 36 artillery battalion, 2 SSM battalions and 5 SAM battalions
Equipment: 1,700+ MBTs and 1,000+ MICVs and APCs; Army Aviation has 11 helicopter squadrons and fixed wing liaison aircraft

Air Force

Personnel: 33,000
Organisation: 10 fighter, 12 fighter ground attack, 1 COIN squadron, 1 recce squadron and 3 transport squadrons together with helicopters, trainers and liaison aircraft

SPAIN

Navy

Personnel: 29,000 including 22,000 conscripts

Fleet: 1 aircraft carrier, 9 frigates, 10 corvettes, 8 submarines, 13 fast attack craft, 12 mine sweepers and amphibious and auxiliary forces. A Maritime Vigilance Force of 1 destroyer, 4 corvettes, 17 patrol boats and 25 smaller craft is deployed for patrol purposes

Naval Aviation

Organisation: 2 fighter ground attack, 6 helicopter and 1 liaison squadron

Marines

Personnel: 11,000
Organisation: 1 brigade, 6 regiments and 1 special operations battalion
Equipment: includes MBTs and APCs

Right: *the current Spanish combat uniform para wings*

Army

Personnel: 181,000 including 112,000 conscripts
Organisation: 6 regional and 2 insular commands comprising 1 armoured division, 1 mechanised division, 1 motorised division and 2 mountain divisions. All divisions have 1 light armoured cavalry regiment, 1 artillery regiment, 1 air defence group, 1 engineer regiment and a logistic support regiment
Equipment: 834 MBTs, 450 armoured cars and 1,735 APCs

Army Aviation

Organisation: 5 helicopter battalions; 1 attack battalion, 1 transport battalion and 3 manoeuvre battalions
Fleet: 190 helicopters

Air Force

Personnel: 35,000
Organisation: 3 regional commands, Central Air Command (1st Military); Straits Air Command (2nd Military) and Eastern Air Command (3rd Military), plus Air Command, Canary Islands. Straits Air Command

Left: *a Spanish Army patch*

The Legion rank breast patch of a group leader, Spain

comprises 1 fighter wing with two squadrons, 1 fighter ground attack wing with 2 squadrons, 1 fighter ground attack training wing with 2 squadrons, 1 ASW maritime patrol wing, Air Academy and 1 helicopter training wing with 3 squadrons

SRI LANKA

Navy
Personnel: 9,200
Fleet: 3 command ships, 21 FACs, 46 patrol craft, 2 survey craft and other amphibious vessels

Army
Personnel: 70,000
Organisation: 3 divisional HQs, 9 infantry brigades, 2 recce regiments, 5 task force groups, 1 artillery regiment, 1 air defence regiment, 4 engineer regiments, 1 commando regiment and 1 special forces battalion
Equipment: 50 MBTs, 31 armoured cars and 200+ APCs; Army Aviation operates 1 squadron

The Sudanese Army cap badge

Air Force
Personnel: 700
Organisation: 1 COIN, 1
interceptor attack, 2
transport, 3 helicopter and 1
trainer squadron

SUDAN

Navy
Personnel: 500
Fleet: 11 patrol craft

Army
Personnel: 60,000
Organisation: 6 regional
commands, 1 armoured
division HQ, 1 airborne corps
HQ, 1 republican guard
brigade, 2 armoured brigades,
14 infantry brigades, 1
parachute brigade, 3 artillery
battalions, 2 air defence
brigades, 1 SAM battalion, 1
engineer battalion, 1 ranger
company and 1 special
operations counter terrorist
unit
Equipment: 173 MBTs, 120
armoured cars and 205 APCs

Air Force
Personnel: 3,000
Organisation: 2 interceptor
FGA, 3 FGA, 1 COIN, 1
transport and 1 helicopter
squadron

SURINAME

Navy
Personnel: 300
Fleet: 16 craft

Army
Personnel: 2,800
Organisation: 3 battalions,
infantry, support and military
police, plus a mechanised
cavalry unit
Equipment: 30 AFVs

Air Force
Personnel: 100
Organisation: 7 fixed and 3
rotary wing aircraft

SWEDEN

Navy
Personnel: 9,150 including 6,500

conscripts
Fleet: 12 submarines, 6 corvettes, 28 fast attack craft, 8 patrol craft, 34 mine layers, 7 mine hunters, 16 mine sweepers, amphibious and auxiliary forces. Naval Aviation comprises 3 helicopter squadrons with 28 helicopters

Army
Personnel: 35,000 including 27,000 conscripts
Organisation: 6 divisional HQs, 2 armoured brigades, 3 mechanised brigades, 6 infantry brigades, 5 Norrland (Arctic warfare) brigades, plus 75 independent infantry, artillery and anti-aircraft battalions deployed in 24 local defence districts
Equipment: 780 MBTs and 707 APCs; Army Aviation comprises 1 battalion of 4 helicopter transport companies and 2 helicopter anti-tank companies with a total of 71 helicopters

Air Force
Personnel: 7,600 including 4,600 conscripts
Organisation: 7 wings, each with 2-3 squadrons. Combat squadrons include 5 ground attack, 1 light attack, 10 fighter interceptor and 3 recce fighter

SWITZERLAND

Total active manpower is 3,400 regular servicemen, but the militia system whereby eligible manpower receives 4 months' recruit training with refresher periods of 3 weeks over 8 years until age 32, and 6 weeks over 3 years until age 42, provides mobilisation within 48 hours for the figures quoted below

Army
Personnel: 400,000 (on mobilisation) from 1995, under *Armée 95* reorganisation
Organisation: under *Armée 95* 4 Field Army Corps (including

A Swiss medical unit working for the UN

current Air Corps), 4 territorial divisions and 2 territorial brigades
Equipment: 920 MBTs, 1,350 APCs and 310 tank destroyers; the marine section of the Army Corps has 11 patrol craft

Air Corps
Personnel: 45,000 (on mobilisation)
Organisation: operates as the Fifth Army Corps, and includes 1 air force brigade with 3 regiments, 1 air field brigade with 3 regiments and 1 air defence brigade with 8 anti-aircraft regiments. There are 25 squadrons in total, each with 12 aircraft

SYRIA

Navy
Personnel: 4,000
Fleet: 6 submarines, 2 corvettes, 19 missile fast attack craft, 8 patrol craft and 10 mine sweepers; Naval Aviation has a fleet of 36 helicopters

Army
Personnel: 300,000 including 150,000 conscripts
Organisation: 3 corps HQs with 5 armoured divisions each with 2 armoured brigades; 3 mechanised infantry divisions each with 1 armoured and 2 mechanised infantry brigades, 6 independent brigades, 6 artillery brigades, 7 paratroop brigades and 10 commando battalions
Equipment: 4,020 MBTs, 1,200 armoured cars and 3,500 AIFVs and APCs

Air Force
Personnel: 60,000
Organisation: 2 strike, 18 fighter, 8 fighter ground attack, 1 recce, 2 transport, 3 helicopter attack and helicopter transport squadrons

Air Defence Command
Personnel: 60,000
Organisation: 21 brigades

TAIWAN

Navy
Personnel: 35,000
Fleet: 24 destroyers, 8 frigates, 3 corvettes, 54 FACs, 55 patrol craft, 4 submarines, 3 mine hunters, 21 mine sweepers and other amphibious vessels; Naval Aviation operates 32 fixed and 24 rotary wing aircraft

Marines
Personnel: 35,000
Organisation: 2 divisions
Equipment: 110 MBTs, 700 light tanks, AIFVs and APCs

TANZANIA

Navy
Personnel: 800
Fleet: 16 patrol craft and 6 other vessels

Army
Personnel: 42,000
Organisation: 3 divisional HQs, 1 armoured and 8 infantry brigades, 6 artillery batteries, 2 ATk, 1 SAM, 2 signals, 1 engineer and 1 commando battalion
Equipment: 86 MBTs, 24 armoured cars and 80 APCs

Air Force
Personnel: 1,000
Organisation: 3 fighter, 1 transport and 1 helicopter squadron plus 6 trainer aircraft

A Taiwanese commando patch

Army
Personnel: 270,000
Organisation: 3 army HQs, 6 corps HQs, 2 armoured divisions, 2 mechanised infantry divisions, 10 heavy infantry divisions, 6 light infantry divisions, 2 airborne brigades, 1 special forces command, 1 SSM battalion and 4 SAM batteries
Equipment: 1,270 MBTs and 1,400 APCs; Army Aviation operates a fleet of 103 helicopters

Air Force
Personnel: 72,000
Organisation: 21 fighter ground attack, 2 interceptor, 1 recce, 1 CAS night attack and 7 transport squadrons, plus 122 helicopters and 200+ trainers

THAILAND

Navy
Personnel: 46,000
Fleet: 12 frigates, 3 corvettes, 9 FACs, 31 patrol craft, 26 fisheries protection vessels, 37 river patrol craft, 11 mine sweepers and other amphibious forces; Naval Aviation operates 2 MP and ASW, 1 maritime patrol and SAR, 1 maritime patrol strike and 1 helicopter squadron

Above: *the Thailand Free Fall parachute team*
Below: *the Thailand Navy para wings*

Marines
Personnel: 20,000
Organisation: 2 divisions with 6 infantry regiments, 1 artillery regiment and 1 amphibious battalion
Equipment: 40 LVTPs

Army
Personnel: 190,000
Organisation: 1 cavalry division, 2 armoured divisions, 1 artillery division, 1 anti-aircraft artillery division, 7 infantry divisions, 1 special warfare command, 8 independent infantry battalions, 11 engineer regiments, 4 recce companies and 5 aviation companies
Equipment: 584 MBTs, 32 armoured cars and 1,890 APCs; Army Aviation operates liaison and light transport aircraft, together with nearly 200 helicopters

Air Force
Personnel: 43,000
Organisation: 3 fighter, 1 fighter ground attack, 7 COIN and light attack, 1 recce, 3 transport and 2 helicopter squadrons, together with trainer and liaison aircraft

TOGO

Navy
Personnel: 100
Fleet: 2 patrol craft

Army
Personnel: 4,650
Organisation: 2 infantry regiments, 1 presidential guard regiment, 1 para commando regiment of battalion size and 1 support regiment
Equipment: 12 MBTs, 55 armoured cars and 34 APCs

Air Force
Personnel: 250
Organisation: 1 COIN light attack squadron plus 4 helicopters and 9 transport liaison aircraft

TRINIDAD AND TOBAGO

Coast Guard
Personnel: 750
Fleet: 13 patrol craft, plus 1 fixed and 2 rotary wing aircraft

Army
Personnel: 2,000
Organisation: 2 infantry battalions and 1 commando platoon

Air Wing
Personnel: 50
Fleet: 1 fixed and 1 rotary wing

TUNISIA

Navy
Personnel: 4,500
Fleet: 1 frigate, 5 fast attack craft, 12 patrol craft and 2 attack craft

Army
Personnel: 27,000 including 24,000 conscripts
Organisation: 2 mechanised brigades, 1 desert brigade with 3 regiments, 1 anti-aircraft artillery brigade, 3 artillery, 1 engineer and 1 armoured recce regiments and 4 para commando battalions
Equipment: 76 MBTs, 54 tank destroyers, 70 armoured cars and 138 APCs; Army Aviation has a fleet of 33 helicopters

Air Force
Personnel: 3,500
Organisation: 1 fighter ground attack recce, 1 light attack training and 1 COIN training squadron, and other aircraft including transport, liaison, training and helicopters

TURKEY

Navy
Personnel: 50,900 including 40,000 conscripts
Fleet: 12 destroyers, 8 frigates, 15 submarines, 18 fast attack craft, 28 patrol craft, 7 mine layers and 26 mine sweepers, plus other amphibious forces and auxiliaries

Naval Aviation
Personnel: 900
Organisation: 1 ASW and 1 helicopter squadron

Army
Personnel: 470,900 including 425,000 conscripts
Organisation: 4 armies with 10 corps HQs; 1 mechanised and 13 infantry divisions; 7 armoured, 6 mechanised, 10 infantry, 1

Below: *a Turkish para commando patch*

A Ugandan Army cap badge

airborne and 2 commando brigades

Equipment: 3,800 + MBTs and 3,500 + APCs; further MBTs, APCs and tank destroyers are being procured. Army Aviation operates both fixed and rotary wing aircraft

Air Force

Personnel: 57,000 including 32,000 conscripts

Organisation: fighter ground attack aircraft number over 500, including F-16s, F-4Es and F-5As; interceptors number 180 including F-4s and F-104s and the Air Force also has recce, transport and training aircraft, along with ECM and SAR helicopters

UGANDA

Army

Personnel: 75,000

Organisation: 6 infantry brigades

Equipment: 4 MBTs and 28 APCs; there is a naval fleet of 6 patrol boats under army direction, and an air force, also under army direction, of 100 personnel with 15 helicopters and 7 trainers

UNITED ARAB EMIRATES

Navy

Personnel: 1,900

Fleet: 2 corvettes, 8 missile

FACs and 9 patrol craft, together with other amphibious forces. The coast guard has a fleet of 45 coastal patrol boats and craft. Naval Aviation has a fleet of 2 fixed and 7 rotary wing aircraft

Army

Personnel: 40,000
Organisation: 1 royal guard brigade, 1 armoured brigade, 2 infantry brigades with 9 battalions, 1 mechanised brigade with 5 armoured car battalions, 3 artillery battalions (equal to brigade strength), 1 air defence brigade and 1 ranger battalion
Equipment: 211 MBTs, 166 operational armoured cars and 414 APCs

Air Force

Personnel: 1,500
Organisation: 3 fighter ground attack, 2 light attack training and 1 recce squadron plus training, transport, helicopter and air defence operations

UNITED KINGDOM

Navy

Personnel: 51,000 after reductions, including 3,400 Womens' Royal Naval Services
Fleet: 3 ASW carriers, 12 destroyers, 3 ballistic missile submarines (nuclear), 13 submarines (nuclear), 4 patrol submarines, 27 frigates, 14 landing craft, 13 MCMVs, 3 mine hunters, 17 mine sweepers, plus numerous light forces and auxiliaries

Naval Aviation

Organisation: 3 shipborne fighter, 9 ASW helicopter, 3 commando assault, 1 AEW helicopter, 3 air crew training, 2 fleet support and SAR squadrons, 1 fleet training and support unit and 1 support unit

Royal Marines

Personnel: 4,000
Organisation: 1 commando brigade HQ, 3 commando units, 1 commando artillery regiment and 1 artillery battery, 2 engineer and 1 light helicopter squadron, 1 logistic regiment and 1 Special Boat Service

Army

Personnel: 116,000 after reductions, plus the Ulster Defence Regiment (6,300) and Territorial Army (63,500)
Organisation: 1 corps HQ, 3 armoured divisions, 1 infantry division, 1 air mobile brigade, 1 mechanised brigade, 3 infantry brigades and 11 territorial brigades (not fully manned). After reduction, this will leave 8 armoured regiments

Above: *the badge of the UK Army Air Corps*

Above right: *the 7th Duke of Edinburgh's Own Gurkha Rifles*

(battalions), 2 armoured recce regiments (battalions), 1 training cadre armoured regiment, 38 infantry and mechanised infantry battalions including 2 Gurkha, 12 artillery regiments including 3 MLRS, 3 air defence regiments and 10 engineer regiments.

The planned ACE Rapid Reaction Corps (ARRC) will comprise European troops under UK command, and consist of 1 armoured division based in Germany, 1 infantry division based in the UK and 1 air mobile brigade. It will total 55,000 personnel. The UK Support Command (Germany) comprises ex-BAOR Forces, which totalled 56,000 in 1992 and which were neither transferred to ARRC nor disbanded. Other forces deployed overseas include: **Belize** 1,300 personnel; 1 armoured recce troop, 1 field artillery battery, 1 engineer squadron, 1 infantry battalion and 1 flight Army Air Corps (AAC)
Brunei 800 personnel; 1 Gurkha infantry battalion and 1 flight

Army Air Corps
Cambodia military observers and mine clearance personnel, under UN direction
Canada 1 training unit
Cyprus 2,300 personnel; 1 armoured recce and 1 engineer support squadron, 2 infantry battalions and 1 flight Army Air Corps
Falklands 1,000 personnel; 1 engineer field squadron and 1 infantry group
Gibraltar 770 personnel; Gibraltar regiment
Hong Kong 5,500 personnel; 1 Gurkha engineer regiment, 1 Gurkha signal regiment, 1 UK infantry battalion, 3 Gurkha infantry battalions and 1 squadron Army Air Corps
Sinai MFO detachment
Equipment: 1,198 MBTs, about 1,000 armoured cars, about 4,000 AIFVs, APCs and other AFVs. The Army Air Corps fleet extends to about 350 helicopters

Air Force
Personnel: 71,000 after reductions
Organisation: 9 strike attack, 6 ground attack, 3 maritime patrol ASW, 2 recce and 1 photo recce squadrons, 7 air defence, 13 transport, 1 AEW, 2 tanker and 2 SAR squadrons, the Queen's Flight and training

A UK parachute regiment badge

Overseas deployment of RAF squadrons:
Belize 1 fixed and 1 rotary wing aircraft flight
Canada 1 detachment fixed wing
Cyprus 1 helicopter squadron and 1 squadron RAF regiment
Falklands 1 helicopter squadron, 1 fixed wing flight and 1 transport flight
Germany 4 cut to 3 squadrons
Hong Kong 1 helicopter squadron

UNITED STATES OF AMERICA

Navy
Personnel: being reduced from 536,000 to 501,000
Atlantic Command (comprising the Second Fleet, Atlantic Sixth Fleet and Mediterranean Fleet), HQ Norfolk, Virginia: **fleet** 7 aircraft carriers, 230 surface vessels, 60 attack

Insignia of the United States Armed Forces

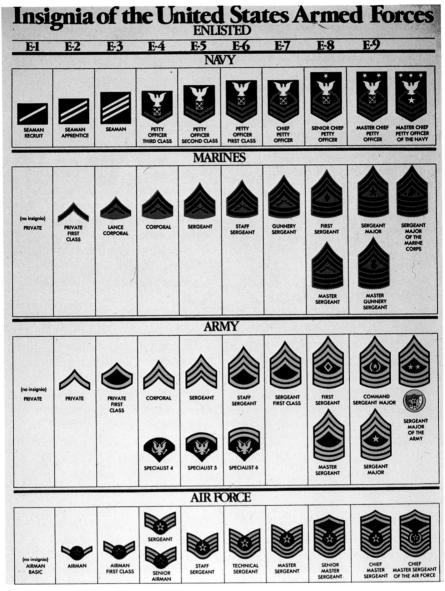

Above: *a chart of enlisted personnel insignia for the US armed forces*

Right: *a chart of insignia for officers of the US armed forces*

Insignia of the United States Armed Forces

OFFICERS

O-1	O-2	O-3	O-4	O-5	O-6	O-7	O-8	O-9	O-10	SPECIAL

NAVY

ENSIGN	LIEUTENANT JUNIOR GRADE	LIEUTENANT	LIEUTENANT COMMANDER	COMMANDER	CAPTAIN	COMMODORE	REAR ADMIRAL	VICE ADMIRAL	ADMIRAL	FLEET ADMIRAL

MARINES

SECOND LIEUTENANT	FIRST LIEUTENANT	CAPTAIN	MAJOR	LIEUTENANT COLONEL	COLONEL	BRIGADIER GENERAL	MAJOR GENERAL	LIEUTENANT GENERAL	GENERAL	

ARMY

SECOND LIEUTENANT	FIRST LIEUTENANT	CAPTAIN	MAJOR	LIEUTENANT COLONEL	COLONEL	BRIGADIER GENERAL	MAJOR GENERAL	LIEUTENANT GENERAL	GENERAL	GENERAL OF THE ARMY

AIR FORCE

SECOND LIEUTENANT	FIRST LIEUTENANT	CAPTAIN	MAJOR	LIEUTENANT COLONEL	COLONEL	BRIGADIER GENERAL	MAJOR GENERAL	LIEUTENANT GENERAL	GENERAL	GENERAL OF THE AIR FORCE

WARRANT

NAVY	MARINES	ARMY	AIR FORCE	COAST GUARD
WARRANT OFFICER — W-1	WARRANT OFFICER	WARRANT OFFICER	WARRANT OFFICER	
CHIEF WARRANT OFFICER — W-2	CHIEF WARRANT OFFICER	CHIEF WARRANT OFFICER	CHIEF WARRANT OFFICER	
CHIEF WARRANT OFFICER — W-3	CHIEF WARRANT OFFICER	CHIEF WARRANT OFFICER	CHIEF WARRANT OFFICER	
CHIEF WARRANT OFFICER — W-4	CHIEF WARRANT OFFICER	CHIEF WARRANT OFFICER	CHIEF WARRANT OFFICER	

Coast Guard enlisted rating badges are the same as the Navy's for grades E-1 through E-6. E-7s through E-9s have silver specialty marks, eagles and stars, and gold chevrons. The badge of the Master Chief Petty Officer of the Coast Guard has a gold chevron and specialty mark, a silver eagle and gold stars. Coast Guard officers use the same rank insignia as Navy officers. For all ranks, the gold Coast Guard shield on the uniform sleeve replaces the Navy star.

Top left: *the Seal of the US Department of Defense*

Centre left: *the US Joint Chiefs of Staff badge*

Bottom left: *the Seal of the US Department of the Navy*

submarines and support vessels

Pacific Command (comprising the Third Fleet, Central, Eastern and Northern Pacific Fleet, Seventh Fleet and Western Pacific Fleet), HQ Pearl Harbor, Hawai'i: **fleet** 6 aircraft carriers, 200 surface combat vessels, 20 attack submarines and support vessels

Combined US Fleet: 14 aircraft carriers, 25 ballistic missile submarines, 90 attack submarines, 46 cruisers, 38 destroyers, 51 frigates, 6 guided missile hydrofoils, 10 coastal patrol craft, 28 mine warfare forces, over 200 amphibious forces and over 300 major auxiliaries

Military Sealift Command: operates 69 active ships and 220 preserved ships, in addition to about 340 US flag ships, which include ocean surveillance ships, oilers and hospital ships

Naval Aviation Organisation: divided into

Naval Air Force Pacific and Naval Air Force Atlantic, with 13 active carrier air wings, 26 fighter, 33 fighter attack, 13 attack, 2 recce, 24 maritime patrol, 11 ASW, 15 AEW, 18 ASW helicopter, 9 EW, 3 mine countermeasures helicopter, 2 communications support, 17 transport and miscellaneous support and 20 squadrons under naval air training command. There are 2 further carrier air wings, under Naval Aviation Reserve, comprising 49 squadrons

Marine Corps
Personnel: 159,000
Organisation: 3 Marine Expeditionary Forces (MEF) with 3 divisions and 3 air wings, 27 infantry battalions, 12 light infantry companies, 2 tank battalions, 3 light armoured infantry battalions, 3 artillery regiments and 5 SAM batteries
Equipment: 221 MBTs, 735 AFVs and 2,400 APCs

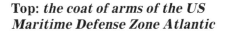

Top: *the coat of arms of the US Maritime Defense Zone Atlantic*

Above: *the US Navy 7th Fleet*

Overleaf, main picture: *the multi-role aircraft carrier* USS America *(CV-66);* inset left: *the offical insignia of the aircraft carrier* USS America; inset right: *the insignia of the Carrier Air Wing 5 (CVW-5)*

79

CARRIER AIR WING

FIVE

Above: *the crest representing the third era of active service for the battleship* USS Iowa *(BB-61)*

Right: *the battleship* USS Iowa *(BB-61); John Giss of Iowa designed the crest for the ship*

Above: *the shoulder patch of the US Fifth Army, 1988*

Below: *the shoulder patch of the US Eighth Army, also 1988*

Coast Guard
Personnel: 38,000
Organisation: Commander Pacific Area is responsible for four districts, including Alaska and Hawai'i; Commander Atlantic Area is responsible for 6 districts, all of which come under Navy control in time of war
Fleet: about 150 ships and 50 fixed and 190 rotary wing aircraft

Marine Aviation
Personnel: 27,000
Organisation: 3 air wings with 2 deployed in continental USA and 1 in the Pacific; 17 fighter attack, 6 fighter ground

attack, 4 ECM, 3 transport, 2
observation, 15 helicopter
assault, 9 helicopter heavy lift
and 6 light helicopter
squadrons

Army
Personnel: being reduced from
618,200 to 536,000
Organisation: moving towards
having 2 corps with 12 active
divisions. One corps has 2
active divisions in Europe and
2 in the Pacific Rim, and one
corps has 8 divisions in the
USA. Overseas divisions
comprise 1st Armored Division
and 3rd Infantry Division in
Europe, the 2nd Infantry
Division in South Korea and

**Above: *the shoulder patch of the
US Army, Europe***

**Below: *the shoulder patch of XI
Corps Artillery, the US Army
National Guard***

85

the 25th Light Infantry Division in Hawai'i. These will be backed by 5 US-based contingency forces divisions. The major active component units are Training and Doctrine Command (HQ Fort Monroe, Virginia); Intelligence and Security Command (USA) (HQ Fort Belvoir, Virginia); Forces Command (USA) (HQ Fort McPherson, Georgia), US Forces Korea (HQ Seoul), US Army Pacific (HQ Fort Shafter, Hawai'i), US Army Europe (HQ USAREUR) and Seventh Army Europe (HQ Heidelberg, Germany), Southern European Task Force (HQ Vicenza, Italy), US Army South (Panama Canal Zone) (HQ Fort Clayton) and US Central Command (HQ McDill Air Force Base).
Equipment: about 19,250 MBTs including those in storage and in reserve, 6,724 MICV CFVs and about 26,000 APCs

Army Aviation
Fleet: about 500 fixed and 9,000 rotary wing aircraft plus a further 3,150 with the Army National Guard

Air Force
Personnel: being reduced from 458,100 to 430,000
Organisation: Air Combat Command (ACC) is responsible for all fighters, attack aircraft, bombers, ballistic missiles, recce and air refuelling assets. This has at its command the 1st Air Force (AF), 2nd AF, 8th AF, 9th AF, 12th AF and 20th AF.

Air Mobility Command (AMC) is responsible for all transport assets. It has at its command the 15th AF, 21st AF and 22nd AF.

Air Material Command comprises Air Force Logistic Command and Air Force Systems Command.

The Pacific Air Forces comprise the 5th AF, 7th AF, 11th AF and 13th AF, and US Air Forces in Europe are the 3rd AF, 16th AF and 17th AF.

In total, there were about 200 wings, which are being cut to 150, and include the following squadrons: 19 ICBM, 17 bombers, 61 fighters, 32 air refuelling, 6 strategic C2, 3 intelligence, 11 special operations force, 3 EW, 9 tactical C2, 21 strategic air lift, 12 tactical air lift, 8 SAR and 2 special missions.
Fleet: the number of aircraft amounts to some 8,500 in total

Right: *the emblem of the 512th Tactical Fighter Squadron, painted on the intake of an F-4 Phantom II aircraft*

Air Force

Personnel: 20,000
Organisation: 5 interceptor regiments, 1 fighter ground attack regiment, 4 transport regiments and 4 helicopter regiments

YEMEN, THE

Navy

Personnel: 2,500 including 500 marines
Fleet: 6 mine sweepers, 13 fast attack craft, 3 patrol craft, 3 mine warfare craft, and other amphibious forces; the marine police operate 9 patrol craft

Army

Personnel: over 50,000
Organisation: based on combined north and south forces; 19 infantry brigades (9 of which have regiment strength), 4 armoured brigades (3 at battalion strength), 2 mechanised, 1 artillery, 1 paratroop, 1 commando and 1 marine brigade, 4 independent tank, 15 artillery, 3 anti-aircraft and 1 SSM brigade
Equipment: 1,200 MBTs, 300 armoured cars and 888 AIFVs and APCs

Air Force

Personnel: 3,500
Organisation: 2 strike attack, 8 fighter ground attack, 1 ground attack, 2 transport and 3 helicopter squadrons

YUGOSLAVIA, FORMER

Navy

Note: the Navy had been staffed mostly by ethnic Slovenians and Croatians. Most vessels are now in the hands of the Serbs, who have no efficient naval bases and no trained personnel to man the vessels
Fleet: 4 frigates, 11 submarines, 13 patrol boats, 15 fast attack craft, 14 torpedo boats, 13 mine sweepers and other amphibious forces

Army

Personnel: prior to the outbreak of fighting in Bosnia, the total personnel was believed to be up to 150,000
Organisation: 23 infantry brigades, 8 tank brigades, 5 mechanised brigades, 1 mountain brigade, 1 airborne brigade, 14 field artillery regiments, 11 anti-aircraft artillery regiments, 6 anti-tank regiments and 4 SAM regiments
Equipment: about 1,100 MBTs, 200 scout cars, 1,000 AIFVs and APCs

Air Force

Personnel: 25,000

Organisation: 3 air corps, of which 1st Air Defence (Combat) comprised 12 fighter bomber, 12 interceptor and 4 recce squadrons

The approximate split of the above former Yugoslavian forces was as follows:

Bosnia-Herzegovenia Serbs, 67,000 men, armaments 300 tanks and 180 AFVs; Croats, 50,000 men; Moslems, 50,000 men

Croatia army personnel, 70,000 men, militia 120,000 men; equipment land 200 tanks and 200 AFVs, sea 8 landing craft, 1 fast attack craft and 1 submarine, air 2 fighters

Macedonia army personnel, 20,000 men; militia 80,000 men

Slovenia army personnel, 15,000 men; equipment, 120 tanks and 20 AFVs

ZAMBIA

Army

Personnel: 21,000
Organisation: 1 armoured regiment, 9 infantry and 1 engineer battalions, 5 artillery batteries and 1 commando company
Equipment: 48 MBTs, 100 armoured cars and 10 APCs

Air Force

Personnel: 1,500
Organisation: 2 fighter ground attack, 1 COIN, 1 transport, 1 liaison and 1 helicopter squadron plus 20 trainers

ZIMBABWE

Army

Personnel: 40,000
Organisation: 7 brigade HQs, 1 armoured regiment, 23 infantry battalions, 2 artillery regiments, 7 engineer squadrons, 3 presidential guard battalions and 1 commando battalion
Equipment: 43 MBTs, 115 armoured cars and 36 APCs

Air Force

Personnel: 1,000
Organisation: 3 fighter ground attack, 1 fighter light attack, 2 COIN light attack, 1 transport, 1 training and 1 helicopter squadron

ABBREVIATIONS

AA: anti-aircraft
AEW: airborne early warning
AF: air force
AFB: air force base
AFV: armoured fighting vehicle
AIFV: armoured infantry fighting vehicle
APC: armoured personnel carrier
ASW: anti-submarine warfare
ATk: anti-tank
AWACS: airborne warning and control system
CFV: combat fighting vehicle
COIN: counter-insurgency
ECM: electronic countermeasures
ECCM: electronic counter-countermeasures
ELINT: electronic intelligence
EW: electronic warfare
FAC: fast attack craft
FGA: fighter, ground attack
ICBM: intercontinental ballistic missile

LCU: landing craft, utility
LCV: landing craft, vehicles
LVTP: landing vehicle, tracked, personnel
MBT: main battle tank
MCM: mine countermeasures
MCMV: mine countermeasures vessel
MFO: multinational force observers
MICV: mechanised infantry combat vehicle
MLRS: multiple launch rocket system
MR: maritime reconnaissance
recce: reconnaissance
SAM: surface to air missile
SAR: search and rescue
SSBN: ballistic missile submarine, nuclear
SSM: surface to surface missile
SSN: submarine, nuclear
USAREUR: USA Army, Europe
V/STOL: vertical/short take off and landing aircraft

Overleaf: *a view of the NATO airborne warning and control system (AWACS) patch on display with the caps of various air forces of the multinational NATO unit, 1982*

ACKNOWLEDGMENTS

Superlaunch Ltd have pleasure in thanking Guy Taylor, London, for special photography; the Department of Defense, Still Media Records Center, Washington DC and the United Nations Picture Archive, New York for their assistance in supplying photographic material; and Andrew Wright, London, for additional artworks.

Below: *an unofficial insignia used by the US Helicopter Mine Countermeasures Squadron 14 (HM-14) during Operation Intense Look, Gulf of Suez, August 1984*

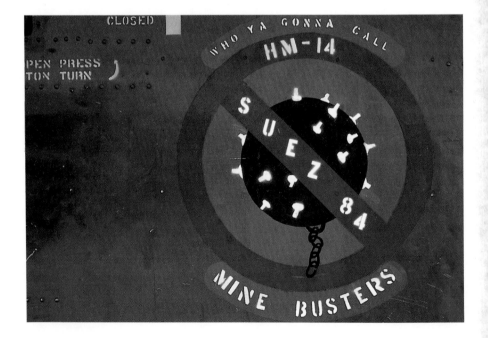